P9-BYX-908

# From Center to Circumference

## *God's Place in the Circle of Self*

Elizabeth-Anne Vanek

PAULIST PRESS
New York / Mahwah, N.J.

The publisher gratefully acknowledges the use of excerpts originally published in *Emmanuel* Magazine, Cleveland, Ohio.

Library of Congress Cataloging-in-Publication Data

Vanek, Elizabeth-Anne, 1951-
   From center to circumference. : God's place in the circle of self / Elizabeth-Anne Vanek.
     p.  cm.
   ISBN 0-8091-3623-6 (alk. paper)
   1. Spiritual life—Catholic Church. 2. Catholic Church—Doctrines. 3. God. 4. Self.  I. Title.
BX2350.V24   1995                       95-35389
248—dc20                                  CIP

Paulist Press
997 Macarthur Boulevard
Mahwah, New Jersey 07430

Printed and bound in the
United States of America

# Contents

# Contents

For my friends
in the company of saints,
especially
**Carroll Stuhlmueller**
who smiles upon us all
and for
Ewert Cousins, Tom Frayne, Tim Hubert,
Lelde Alida Kalmite, Jean Maher, O.S.B. and Stanley Selinger
whose presence in my life
is an ongoing source of courage and joy.

# Introduction

For three decades now we have been enjoying a renaissance of spirituality. In the sixties our secular culture was awakened to spirituality and taught techniques of meditation by gurus and Zen masters coming from the East. Then in the seventies and eighties, we witnessed a return to roots in which Christians and Jews sought to recover their own spiritual heritage. The house of prayer movement mushroomed around the country; centering prayer spread widely; guided retreats became available not only to religious but to the laity as well. Academic programs in spirituality began to appear on university campuses.

In 1978 Paulist Press brought out the first volume in the series The Classics of Western Spirituality. Now over eighty volumes have appeared, providing a solid resource for spiritual reading and study. Thus the renaissance of spirituality has been rich in personal experience and practice, while at the same time being grounded in the knowledge and wisdom of the classical spiritual traditions.

The present book by Elizabeth-Anne Vanek reflects a certain mature phase of this spiritual renaissance. Thoroughly grounded in the classics of the tradition, she has been gifted with a rich spiritual and mystical life of her own. Out of gratitude and humility—and fully aware of the vulnerability of her position—she shares her personal experience with her readers. This sharing can evoke in the readers an awareness of their own experience and its relevance to their spiritual journey. Her wisdom, enhanced by many years as a spiritual director, shines through. The reader will feel the sure and gentle touch of her guiding hand.

At times in the past—for example, in the High Middle Ages in the West—spiritual writers began sharing their own religious experience, sometimes as a direct description and sometimes with the intent of evoking the readers' experience. I believe that we are at such a stage now, which I have called above a mature phase of our spiritual renaissance. Elizabeth-Anne Vanek provides us with a rich example of the dynamics of this phase, which can encourage others to follow in this way.

The spiritual path she provides is at once modern and classical. It is profoundly and explicitly God-centered. This is both challenging and refreshing in an era that has emphasized the human and the psychological dimensions in the spiritual journey. However, far from ignoring these dimensions, she treats them as intimately encompassed by God: "The new call," she says, "was for God to be both center and circumference; the new call was for God to become the totality of myself."

The book leads the reader through the routine of a busy life—through the joys and the tensions of the everyday, as well as intense experiences of the presence of God. Throughout the journey, the reader is guided into a holistic spirituality in which God increasingly becomes both the center and the circumference of the self.

*Ewert Cousins*

# Letter to a Spiritual Director

*Dear Tom,*

You asked me to describe what happens in prayer and I gave a very abbreviated response: "I sit and sometimes nothing happens, even if I sit for an hour." I've thought about this response and realize it was helpful neither for you nor for me. The reason for my reticence was no doubt embarrassment. What happens in prayer is an intimate topic, and yet if I am to teach others how to pray (how presumptuous this sounds) and if I am to write on prayer, then I need to be able to articulate what happens in my own praying. I thought that my poetry—particularly *Woman Dreamer*—was a "coming out," a self-exposé, if you will, but this seems infinitely more risky....

I do "just sit" but a variety of experiences can take place. Sometimes "what happens" is affected by my physical and emotional state, by the self I bring to prayer; sometimes "what happens" is more God's initiative than mine and I simply try to respond to that initiative. The most satisfying experience of prayer happens when I am fully conscious and when God seems to be fully present. Of course, I realize that my feelings have nothing at all to do with whether God is present or not: God is *always* present, but, for one reason or another, we are not always aware of this. At those times when I am most conscious of this Presence, there is a marriage of my desire and God's desire, of my surrender to God's embrace and of God's reaching out to me....

1

There are so many variables and subtle nuances at work that it would be impossible for me to provide neat categories of my prayer experiences. Typically, I do "just sit"—sometimes in response to a definite call to prayer which is irresistible, sometimes because I want to connect with God before bed or early in the morning, sometimes because the events of the day have presented a specific need which I want to articulate in prayer.

When I am tired or unwell, I am aware of the limited presence I bring to God. I choose to spend time with God, knowing that I will very likely drift off into sleep or that I will experience nothing more than a series of distractions. In spite of this, I do sit, believing that my fidelity is more important than what I experience and that by acknowledging my desire to be in union with God, I am giving worship. "Nothing much" may happen in a tangible sense, but I know that I have at least given God the gift of my time; if God chooses to break through my sluggishness, then I am there, waiting. In times of deep exhaustion, I sometimes lie down in my prayer spot (the futon in my study) and ask God to be with me as I sleep, to hold me in my weakness and to communicate to me—through dreams, perhaps—anything that I need to pay attention to. When I commit myself to God's care in this way, I experience myself as a much beloved child, resting within the arms of my God.

There are times both when I am sitting and when I am otherwise occupied (e.g. walking, driving, doing chores, etc.) that I experience a welling up of love which calls me to prayer. Whether this love is my response to God or God's response to me, I am not sure: it just happens. I find myself concentrating on this feeling and turning to a mantra of some kind—something like, "My Lord and my God" or, more recently, "Jesus." The mantra becomes as rhythmic as my breathing—not rote, by any means, but a way of acknowledging the love within without resorting to meaningless babble. In the face of this love, words seem empty; the mantra, on the other hand, gives focus and allows prayer to happen in me, even while I am engaged in outward activities including conversation with others. The prayer continues. This experience is at once joyful and sad. Often, I feel simultaneously empty and full. I taste God's presence but crave for a deeper presence still. I am left knowing that fullness belongs to a time when I have a greater capacity to respond.

Another common way of praying for me is to allow myself to move deeply within into the center of self. I may begin by presenting a situation of concern to God and then move into silence. This is a dark kind of praying—not dark in the sense of depressing, but I descend deep into the mystery where there is both peace and silence; I lose consciousness of the time and place in which I exist in the moment and move into the darkness of God, into unknowing. It is a descent which I experience physically. Often, I feel rather disoriented when I finally emerge, having lost all sense of myself. I return to waking consciousness feeling vulnerable yet empowered; I experience tenderness and new awareness. It is usually difficult for me to resume my ordinary activities following this way of praying; I need "re-entry" time.

In times of profound grieving, my tears become my prayer. I sit with open hands, allowing the tears to fall freely. I speak of my pain and ask God to carry me through, to be my strength, to bring healing, if that is possible. I find the "pit" psalms helpful, or any other biblical texts which name disorientation as the primary response to life. I tend to identify with the Jesus of Gethsemane, and try to imitate him in surrender to what will be. Moments of intense pain, then, become occasions for me to acknowledge my total dependence on God. The pain does not magically disappear with prayer, but there is emotional release and I find comfort in being in solidarity with the sufferings of Christ. An after-effect of such prayer is a new sense of peace.

When I first came to the States and found myself succumbing to acute homesickness and culture shock, I used to pick up my guitar and strum until my finger nails would break. The few chords I knew would reverberate with powerful feelings—feelings that I could not bring to speech. It was as though the only way I could articulate the whole experience of being an alien in a foreign land was through those basic chords; to this day, though I am no more proficient on the guitar than I was twenty-two years ago, I find that music-making—if it can be called that—is a way of demanding that God should hear me. The more impassioned my playing, the more connected to God I feel and the greater the experience of catharsis or release.

The type of praying which is most difficult for me to articulate is when God approaches me directly, intruding into whatever I am doing, whether it be writing or grading papers, sleeping or looking out of a train window. When this happens and I am intellectually engaged in some activity, I typically begin to sense a Presence—an otherness—surrounding me, exercising a gentle pressure, inviting me to allow myself to be fully absorbed in it. The physical pull is too strong for me to resist. I have to put down my pen, or leave my word processor; often, I find myself covering my face with my hands as though overwhelmed by a great light. I don't usually see a light but I feel it and am blinded by it. There is nothing I desire more than to merge fully with this light, to lose my identity in it, to gain Christ's identity, and to experience no differentiation whatsoever. I have few words when Presence comes. I am filled with awe and deep gratitude. I might find myself repeating, "My Lord and my God." Invariably, I invite God to be my life, to use me for God's ends, to purge me of whatever is an obstacle to God fully residing in me. I want to be stripped of all egocentricity; most especially, I want to know how to love God in that moment and in every moment, how to be more loving to others, how to pray. These responses also surface when I experience God as fire. This often happens on consecutive nights, around 2:00 a.m., and lasts anywhere from half an hour to several hours. I wake up, very conscious of God's presence and of a gentle burning which consumes without causing pain, which radiates through me and around me, engulfing me in flames of love. When this first began to happen, I was frightened to move lest I inadvertently put an end to the experience. Now I no longer cling to its duration but rather try to respond as lovingly as possible to God's initiative. I desire to conform entirely to God's will for me and to give myself completely to God.

Following an experience like this, I often feel bereaved. I have heard in prayer that it would be physically impossible for me to encounter God so directly on a regular basis, that I could not stand the intensity for prolonged periods of time. I have also heard that were I permanently caught up in the ecstatic moment, I would not get my work done. This I know to be true: my work seems so insignificant when I am present to God's presence. I resent anything I have to do and want nothing more than to rest in God. Paradoxically, when I do yield to God's presence, I accomplish everything that needs to be done in far less time than I had previously anticipated. Chronos becomes kairos....

I suppose there are other ways in which I pray—experiencing God in the freedom of water when I swim, or in the earth when I work in my garden; the prayer of listening when I play my Taizé tapes in the car, driving to school and back; liturgical prayer.... Perhaps the simplest prayer of all is when I first open my eyes in the morning and find myself saying, "I love you, God."

And so this is my attempt to answer your question, Tom. It's been useful for me to reflect on all this; the process itself has been prayerful. For this, I thank you.

*Liz*

# From Center to Circumference: God's Place in the Circle of Self

Sometime ago, a cryptic sentence surfaced in prayer: "Make me the subject of your prayer, not the object." I puzzled over this for several days. God, after all, was the One to whom I prayed, and that, I assumed, automatically meant that God was the subject of my attentions. It was God's name that I called upon and it was God whom I expected to respond. What, then, was the significance of this instruction? Had I heard incorrectly? Was God, perhaps, mistaken?

As I pondered over these questions, illumination began to set in. For several years, but especially for the previous year, I had been dealing with family crisis. Very often, what I presented in prayer was an outpouring of my feelings. Time after time, I would state what was going on in my life, the effects all this was having on me, and my desire for God's healing intervention. Now, I realized that while I had been faithful to the prayer of petition, to the prayer of grieving, I had not been present to God's needs, to God's heart. Far from being the subject of my prayer, God had become the object—a captive audience whom I expected to listen but not necessarily respond. Seldom did I enter prayer expecting God to be the focus: it had been my own needs, my own pain, which formed my agenda.

This insight brought sadness rather than guilt. I now saw that my praying had become dramatic monologue, that my focus was the state of my heart and not God's, and that in this, both God and I had been the losers. While God had sustained me through the difficulties in which I found myself, I had offered little in return. My capacity for caring about God had been stunted; my imagination was limited by pain; my spiritual energy burned up in grappling with family issues.

Eventually, I was able to move beyond these discoveries and to embrace new possibilities. "Make me the subject of your prayer" became an invitation rather than a reproach. I felt more alive, more aware, more determined to be "available" to God. I sensed a call to focus exclusively on God so that we could move into deeper relationship.

But how was I to respond to this call? I was still preoccupied with the ongoing crisis—or, rather, I should say "crises"—and I felt completely unskilled at being available in the midst of my own concerns. Instead of pouring out problems, however, my new refrain was "O.K., God, so what am I supposed to do?" As I concentrated on being present, I heard that I was trying too hard, and that it would be much simpler than I expected. I was reminded that an invitation is always freely given and is not meant to be a burden. I told myself that because I desired to respond, this desire was itself prayer. And my desire was to live in as complete awareness as is humanly possible and to be as loving as is humanly possible: I desired to delight God....

In the past, I had given much thought to making God the center of my life. I had worked on stripping myself of ego attachments to allow God more room. It seemed, however, that I was being called to a deeper relationship than this. In my imagination, I saw myself as a circle with God as a dot in the center. Gradually, the dot began to expand, losing its clearly defined boundaries, merging with the rest of the circle until center and circumference became one. The new call was for God to be both center and circumference; the new call was for God to become the totality of myself, so that it was indeed God who lived in me and I in God. It was not that I was to stop presenting my own concerns in prayer, but that I needed to pay greater attention to God's need of me. As I discerned what God wanted of me, I felt both humbled and awed, vulnerable yet energized. I was ready to begin my explorations.

# God at the Center

Allowing God central place in one's life in not a simple, one-time decision; rather, it is a radical act of will, grounded in the sense of what God "wills for us," with ongoing ramifications. Though God had always been a major part of my life, it was only about twelve years ago that I consciously began working toward being "God-centered." Prior to that, I was not centered at all. I moved between mountain top experiences and the depths of the darkest pit, seemingly at random. Childhood memories, broken relationships and professional disappointments were guaranteed to destroy equilibrium, sometimes setting me on a downward spiraling course that plunged me into the abyss. My strategy of avoidance was to clutch at meaning, whether through friendships, reading or writing. I avoided mediocrity at all costs and kept frenetically busy. In this way, I told myself, I was an active participant in ultimate meaning, one who knew how to live instead of vegetate.

Reality hit with a vengeance. A series of painful events led me to confront my lifestyle. What I found was that I had come to doubt my capacity to survive the shifting landscape of my experience. The ups and downs were a shock to my system and the highs themselves were founded more on emotional gratification than on spiritual values. Sobered by this discovery, I told myself that unless God were the center of my life, I was "not going to make it."

Looking back, I am not quite sure what I meant by these words. I don't think I was suicidal, but I certainly didn't feel as though there was much to live for. I believed that I would lose myself in depression or that I would become immobilized by the chronic emptiness I so desperately tried to block out. I remember being painfully conscious of how slowly time moved and of how little there was to look forward to.

I was an expert at living in anticipation of future events. As a child growing up on the Mediterranean island of Malta, there was nothing I looked forward to more than the occasional trips to the beach. Because we lived inland, I had to depend on family members to drive me to the seaside until I was old enough to take buses on my own. Day after blisteringly hot day, I "practiced" swimming on my bed, cleaned my snorkeling equipment and lived in anticipation of the next swim. The present moment had no value; meaning existed in future tense.

This pattern accompanied me into adulthood, traveling with me more than five thousand miles from my childhood home. Though I still looked forward to swimming—in lake or pool—I now lived for emotionally intense conversations or for intellectual sharing; I despised the mundane and looked for God in the extraordinary. It was when I "hit bottom" that I realized that something would have to change: I discovered that while I was an expert at talking "about" God, God was not a reality which made a difference to my way of being.

With the desperation of one who knows it's a matter of "sink or swim," I began the hard work of reshaping my spiritual life. I do not give myself the credit for this work; rather, it was as though God unfolded what I *must* do, and that, having no other alternatives, I complied. Accordingly, I scheduled regular prayer time, began seeing a spiritual director, undertook a course of reading inspirational materials, and also found a therapist. Instead of running from the emptiness, I allowed myself to face it and name it. I examined core issues and destructive patterns of behavior. I relived painful memories and tried to accept all the people and events which had affected me, positively and negatively. And, all the while, I asked God to replace my emptiness with the gift of Godself.

There was little consolation or sense of God's presence during this time. I counted the days between one spiritual direction session and the next, between one therapy session and the next, feeling that if I could only "make it" to the next appointment, perhaps I would avoid the abyss for another month. Pain and purging were companions along the way. I was stripped of ego-desires and former attachments and found myself longing for God to become my very life. What I wanted was to live for God and for God only. This alone would give my life meaning. This alone would enable me to move beyond the pit.

# Letting Go To Possess

One of the paradoxes of the spiritual journey is that it is only when we embrace poverty of spirit that we find the fullness of God. So much of early adulthood is occupied with attaining credentials and "getting ahead" that we often lose sight of the fact that there is a different way of living—one in which we let go of material goals and instead try to live out of God's will for us. I am not discrediting credentials or career paths—they *are* necessary— but to live out of God's will, to find happiness in God's dream for us, is very different from simply forging ahead as though we are in complete control. If God is truly the center and circumference of our lives, then that should make a difference to the kinds of choices we make and the values we hold.

Before my "spiritual conversion," my career path had basically got me nowhere. Having abandoned the idea of a Ph.D. to be home with the children, I taught part-time for several institutions, ran a writers' group, was involved in liturgy planning on a volunteer basis and did free-lance writing and editing. In spite of all my efforts, for ten years my annual salary never exceeded $6,000. My attempts at publishing fiction were, for the most part, fruitless; my articles for religious journals brought in little; my prospects for full-time employment seemed dim; and editorial work did nothing for my soul. I felt frustrated and directionless.

In addition, these twelve years were filled with strings of

professional setbacks and disappointments. Breaking into print was a formidable task—I received seventy-four rejection slips for my first book of poetry alone, and the seventy-fifth—a letter of acceptance—I tossed into the garbage can because I assumed it was negative. Then there were manuscripts lost in the mail, public presentations with my name left off the program or with inaccurate room listings, poems printed with lines out of sequence, and, worse still, a dramatic Advent reading at Notre Dame University, involving an entourage of ten musicians and readers, which nobody attended because of poor advertising.

The final blow came when the publication of my second book—*Extraordinary Time*—was delayed so many months that I missed all scheduled promotional events. I remember looking intently out of my study window each time the UPS truck passed by, hoping that it would be carrying the copies I had ordered for my own use. So obsessed was I with this waiting that I began to live for the arrival of the UPS truck; it was all I thought about. The day came when the UPS driver finally rang my doorbell, presenting me with the long-awaited box. Trembling with anticipation, I tore off the tape and pushed aside the styrofoam chips: to my dismay, I discovered that the cover of each book had been smudged in production. I could neither sell the books nor give them away.

My rage over this event, my frustration over all the preceding incidents, and my disbelief that things would ever go according to plan led me to some soul-searching. Why had writing taken on so much importance in my life? Why was it so easy to place meaning in a box of books and not in day-to-day existence? And if locating meaning outside myself was so painful, how could I focus inward? Intellectually, I could diagnose my spiritual malaise, but I was by no means convinced that I could turn around patterns and attitudes that were so ingrained. I realized that much of my obsession with "being published" stemmed from the need I had as a child "to prove myself." Moving from diagnosis to healing would be no small undertaking.

Instinct told me that what was called for was a ritual of detachment to strengthen me in my resolve to "let go." On my birthday—the winter solstice—I invited a small group of friends to join me and my family for a festival of light. They were not to bring gifts; rather, I asked them to bring an Advent reading, a birthday blessing and a symbol of something in their own lives which they needed to let go. After the readings, I spoke for a few minutes about the setbacks with my writing which had taken on larger-than-life proportions and how oppressed I had allowed myself to become. In front of the assembly, I pledged that from then on, I would never allow the inadequacies of the publishing world to affect my inner life; from then on, I would use my gifts for God's glory, not my own. With that, I placed a defective copy of *Extraordinary Time* in the fireplace, inviting the others present to burn a symbol of their own negative darkness. When the last charred fragments had disappeared, we lit candles from the flames and I received the words of blessing each friend had brought me.

This ritual of detachment gave me the courage to move beyond my own wants and to abandon the outcome of my work to God. What I **did** would no longer be determined by my own willfulness, but by an openness to whatever God might be calling me to. What I **wrote** would depend exclusively upon those words God wanted to reveal through me, and not merely upon my delight in playing with words and meanings or in seeing my name in print. And when I accepted a speaking engagement, it would be for the sake of God's reign, and not for the sake of my ego. In the letting go, I not only made room for God, but allowed new doors of possibility to open. Because my hands were no longer clenched in anger, because they no longer clutched at success, I was free to receive the gifts God wanted to shower on me.

Recently, I have been able to take this resolve to a deeper level. Since that eventful birthday, I have, for the most part, been faithful to this "letting go." At the same time, however, my professional life has been shaped by family needs so that choices about full-time employment and free-lance ministry have been influenced by practical considerations such as income and security. Now that the children are in college, I sense that I am being called to consider more options for myself in terms of my ministry and that this is the time for dreaming—not just **my** dream but God's dream for me. Different possibilities have emerged, and rather than immediately dismiss them as being "risky," I have allowed myself to play with these possibilities and to imagine what it would be like, should they materialize. There is a new conviction, deep within, that if I hear God's call—however impractical—and respond, the bills **will** be paid and all will be well—for all of us. In this awareness, I experience freedom and a real readiness to "go" when the call comes. I feel the inner joy which comes when one can say, "Here I am, Lord," and mean it.

# Surrender

The word "surrender" tends to conjure up negative associations for the western world. Often, when I suggest that God may be inviting someone to a place of surrender, the person I am working with shudders involuntarily before giving any number of reasons to explain why I am probably mistaken. The truth is that the concept of "surrender" is the antithesis of all we have been conditioned to become. From birth on, we have been trained to identify our needs and wants and to go after them. Our culture has schooled us in competitiveness and ambition, in assertiveness and immediate gratification. Even the idea of turning ourselves over to the governance of a higher power—or of recognizing that we are in God's hands—is too radical for most people's comfort. On the surface, surrender and self-fulfillment seem to be contradictions.

In my own journey, I have learned that when I go after what I think I want, the way is fraught with difficulties. When I blindly pursue that which I think will bring me happiness, emptiness persists. When I act as though I can will the right opportunities to present themselves, disappointment is a certainty. What I "want," "pursue," or "will" is not wrong in itself, but it is my basic attitude that is problematic: it is an attitude which suggests that I have control over my destiny, that I can make decisions without paying attention to where God may be calling me.

Sometimes, we prefer not to hear God's call. We imagine that what God calls us to will go against what we dream for ourselves.

We suspect that we will be asked to do the impossible or will be told to give up all that we cherish, all that we have worked or lived for. And, occasionally, we are right: God does indeed intrude into life the way we know it, suggesting a second or third career, a new relationship, a radically different way of thinking or being or spending our time. Life can be turned upside down; nothing remains the same.

The irony is that what God calls us to is always life-giving. The paths we are invited to leave behind yield to paths of greater possibility. The doors we are urged to close are smaller than the doors which open before us. The rooms we are asked to vacate make way for mansions of inestimable size and value.

Of course, I am speaking symbolically here, not of material gains. The way I see it, God continually invites us to greater consciousness, to greater freedom and to more opportunities for loving. When we discern God's call, when we surrender to God's will, then we find our truest happiness. Surrender is not so much a question of "giving up" but of "receiving more"—if we only dare take the risk. Those things we leave behind us, precious though they may have been, are often realities which we have outgrown or which stop us from growing.

But while I believe that the fruit of surrender is life in abundance, I also believe that we need to surrender for God's sake, without motives of gain. To hear God's call and to calculate whether to follow it on the basis of what we will get out of it seems more spiritually deadening than to ignore the call altogether. Surrender in its purest form means turning ourselves over to God unconditionally, praying, "Your will be done in me, on earth, as it is in heaven." It involves basing our decisions on our love for God rather than on self-love. It is characterized by gratitude for the past, rather than by expectations of future gifts. It convinces us to choose life at every opportunity, even though it would be easier to go along with what is rote and predictable. We find ourselves swimming with the current rather than against it;

# DePaul prof stirs controversy at parliament

Cape Town, South Africa (CNS) — A lecture at the World Parliament of Religions in Cape Town by a staff member of DePaul University, Chicago, drew angry protests from some Christian groups.

Elizabeth-Anne Stewart, a faculty member in the religious studies department and campus minister at the Catholic institution, said the controversy over her lecture, "Holy Foolishness: A Christological Paradigm for the New Millennium," took her by surprise. The lecture was based on her book "Jesus the Holy Fool."

At the Dec. 1 opening of the parliament, fundamentalist Muslim and Christian

Elizabeth-Anne
Stewart

groups protested the meeting, some brandishing placards denouncing the parliament for calling Jesus a holy fool.

"I was afraid there would be violence," Stewart said Dec. 6, adding that she found it "perturbing" that people had formed judgments without knowing what her talk was about.

"There is a tradition of holy foolishness that goes back 2,000 years," Stewart said, noting that the term referred to those who "live by different standards to those espoused by the world."

Stewart said the lecture hall was full for her Dec. 4 presentation and she was "warmly received."

"A woman in the front row got up after I had spoken and apologized on behalf of all South Africans for the protesters," said Stewart, one of 42 of DePaul's faculty and students at the parliament. "That was so nice."

*buildings*
*and work*
*for those u*
*Above G*
Bur

instead of struggling furiously, we float effortlessly to where we were meant to be all along.

For me, a significant image of surrender is to rest in God's hand. I once fashioned this hand out of clay. Within it, I molded a figure of a small child, curled up in fetal position, umbilical cord extending from its navel, around the thumb of the hand. This sculpture, crude though it was, captured the essence of how God cherishes each of us and how our very life depends on God's continuing care. Such a God is not saying "surrender or else!" but "come to me and find all that you are seeking, all that will bring healing, all that will set you free...."

More recently, I have been captivated by a small statue in a friend's office; made of unpretentious stone, it depicts Jesus surrounded by children of varying sizes. "Which one is you?" Tim asked as I gazed upon it for the first time. "Why, the child on his lap, of course!" I said, without further thought. Completely at ease, the child leans back in Jesus' arms and, looking up at him trustingly, strokes his beard with one hand. In the place of privilege, in the place of contentment, she is completely safe; secure in his love, she feels the beat of his heart, the warmth of his embrace....

# Cutting Ties

The greatest obstacles to allowing God centrality in our lives are our attachments. When Jesus said, "It is more difficult for the rich to enter the kingdom of heaven than for a camel to go through the eye of a needle" (Lk 19:24), I don't believe he was referring only to the propertied or wealthy. Possessions, of course, do get in the way of a simple lifestyle, but there are other forms of riches which can also be liabilities. A graduate student may live in abject poverty, but if he or she lives exclusively for acquiring more and more knowledge, then there is a subtle form of idolatry at play. A scientist may be devoted to finding a cure for some devastating disease—AIDS, for example—but if that scientist defers thinking about God until the cure is found, then again vocational work has replaced spiritual work in importance. A minister may devote his or her time to building a new church in a poor community, but if fund-raising takes on greater importance than being the spiritual leader of that community, attachments have again got in the way of relationship with God. So often, we justify our attachments on the basis of our motives and of the outcomes we achieve; anything, however, which replaces God at the center of our consciousness is an obstacle on the spiritual path: instead of serving God, we serve lesser gods— "knowledge," "science," "evangelism"....

Just as our activities can stand between ourselves and God, so can our relationships. Ideally, friendships lead us into deeper communion with each other: those we love mirror the divine reality and so draw us closer to the One they reflect. In our humanness, however, we can forget that the friend is only a reflection of God and instead invest ultimate meaning in the relationship. In his epic poem *Paradise Lost* (Book IV L. 299), John Milton writes of Adam and Eve, "He for God only, she for God in him"; that is, that Adam was created for direct relationship with God while Eve had access to God through Adam. While the inequality of the sexes was a given for this seventeenth century poet, today there would be few women or men who would agree with his claim. I quote Milton because, gender issues aside, it is so easy to turn to another as a "god substitute" instead of building our own relationship with God. Sometimes this involves trying to live one's spiritual life vicariously through another whom we assume has a "direct line to God." Clergy, religious, teachers and counselors can easily become "God substitutes" because we imagine they understand the secrets of life. The distortion here is that the "helper" can become the obstacle, particularly if the "helper" is hooked into our attentions by ego needs. We need to run from "would-be gurus," and to check our own hearts when the inclination to be a guru surfaces. A popular Buddhist saying is, "If you meet the Buddha on the path, kill him." In other words, anyone we assume to be the embodiment of perfection or wisdom can be seriously detrimental in our own quest for enlightenment.

Another distortion can happen in a more "equal" relationship when both parties involved trigger intellectual excitement in each other through their God-centered discussions: intellectual excitement in itself is good, but when it becomes a substitute for relationship with God, then, it, too, has taken on idolatrous overtones. The feelings of intimacy that can also be generated by such discussions may delude participants into imagining that they are growing closer to God whereas, in fact, each is enjoying his or her own reflection in the other. Experience tells me that God can be very patient with such a relationship but that, ultimately, God is a jealous God and will eventually reveal the inadequacies of this type of friendship.

John of the Cross writes, "it makes little difference whether a bird is tied by a thin thread or by a cord. For even if tied by a thread, the bird will be prevented from taking off, just as surely as if it were tied by a cord" (*Ascent of Mount Carmel*. Book 1. Chpt. 11:4). I take these words very seriously because I have known, in my own life, what it is to let "work" or "friendship" tie me down. For others, possessions or attitudes may be the threat that impedes them on the journey. Whatever it is, unless we allow God to cut the thread, we will never be able to take flight and soar toward those heights to which God beckons us. Whether made of humble hemp or the finest spun gold, a cord is a cord.

# Dry Wood

In one of my poems, I write about the experience of being "whittled away like dry wood under a skilled carver's knife." In the process of learning how to surrender to God, in the process of letting go of our attachments, we are changed; something so radical begins to happen to us that we find we are not the same person we used to be.

For me, the experience *did* feel like a "carving." No longer in control or *assuming* I was in control, I became entirely passive while God worked upon me. It was a painful process. To be trimmed of superfluities and pared to the core, to see the shavings of my life lie at my feet left me strangely naked. There was nothing to hide behind, nothing to distract me, nothing to pretend. A vast emptiness lay before me. I endured the stripping, unaware of the gifts it would bring. All I could see ahead was pain and darkness and more pain. I feared that I was about to topple into the abyss and that there would be no last-minute rescue act to save me from the fatal plunge. I was taken apart, piece by piece, dismembered and reassembled—emotionally speaking, that is— uncertain whether the pieces would ever fit together properly again or whether they would "work." I began to lose all sense of the jumbled wants, needs, fears, resentments and disappoint- ments that had formerly constructed the "I" that I was. The only reality was the true self which began to emerge under the singing blade. Stripped, refined and given new form, I stepped out of the block of wood, quivering like a newborn creature that has just left the safety of the womb. And everything had changed....

In my newness, I saw things differently, heard things differently and felt differently. All my senses seemed to be heightened, my ways of knowing had become more encompassing, my capacity for compassion had intensified, my creativity was exploding.... I could no longer define myself by my various roles—by what I *did*—but only by what I had become. I could no longer think of future in terms of "goals," "strategies" and "security," but only as it related to the unfolding of God's dream for me. I could no longer approach life as a limited opportunity for exercising my gifts, but instead found myself passionately committed to empowering others. No longer ruled by attachments, I experienced an incredible sense of liberation—a holy indifference as to whom I did (or did not) impress, as to what I did (or did not) accomplish, as to what I did (or did not) own.

As I began to realize who I had become, I was filled with awe. It was rather like seeing myself in a mirror clearly for the first time and realizing that all previous images had been shadowy distortions. Physically, I looked the same, but the essence of my true self (which I name the Christ-self) shone through. Instead of reaching out to a transcendent God, I found God residing fully in the center of myself.

This purging, however, is not a once-in-a-lifetime event, but a continuing reality. Much as I would like to think that the purgative experience is over and done with and that I can move on to a state of permanent union with the divine, the reality is that I, like most people I know, have "unfinished business" to grapple with. Though I hope that the bulk of this work is behind me, I know only too well the memories that still scar my psyche, the issues which can still derail me emotionally. Often, when I find myself caught up in painful events, I realize that God has not finished with me yet, that the holy work of ego-stripping will peel away more and more of my imperfections until that time when **only** the Christ-self is left.

# God Only

Inner pain has been a constant theme in my life. Chronic loneliness, experiences of rejection and a disbelief that the future could hold anything positive for me were all part of my growing up years. As a product of two cultures—British and Maltese—I fitted in nowhere, but my sense of alienation ran deeper than a mixed ethnic background and than always being the "foreigner" wherever I have lived. Looking back, I realize that my inner self was struggling to emerge, struggling to discover itself, in contexts that failed to recognize the validity of such a struggle. Values of attaining higher consciousness, of becoming fully individuated, of moving into union with God were not topics of everyday conversation—or of conversation at all, for that matter. Structures of school, church and family did not offer the tools I so desperately needed for my "inner work." There were no books to chart the path, no role models to follow. I did not even have the vocabulary to describe my inner longings. Deep inside, I knew that my inner life was more important than anything else, but I did not know what to do with this knowledge.

I realized I was a "foreigner" in more ways than one. In Malta, those around me seemed completely absorbed in the material world—in what they owned, in what their families owned, in what they hoped to inherit. Self-definition was based on what one's father "did" for a living and what profession his father had practiced before him. At that time, society was highly stratified, and women of the upper classes were viewed as accessories whose responsibilities were confined to the domestic realm. I do not recall ever hearing women engaged in meaningful conversations or having their ideas valued. "Women's talk" was small-talk, gossip. At precisely the point when conversation began to become interesting, they were expected to leave the dinner table and leave men to their cigars and cognac, while they retreated to the "powder room." I have bitter memories of not being listened to, and, worse still, of having my ideas negated. Even on return visits more than twenty years later, I find that sexism still prevails: few show an interest in my professional life; I am defined only by having husband and children. Ironically, on a recent visit with my son, Peter, then eighteen, I witnessed him being accorded more respect than I, his parent. While he enjoyed adult status and scotch on the rocks on demand, I found myself relegated to kitchen and nursery.

As an adult living five thousand miles away from my childhood home, I still carry scars. Most of the time they are comfortably scabbed over, but when they break open, the pain is excruciating. Though today I would never describe myself as "lonely," there are very few people with whom I can share what is most significant to me. Often, I am perceived as "too intense" or "eccentric"; often, people I expect to understand look at me blankly or else become threatened, even hostile.

Increasingly, I am turning to God for comfort; I remind myself that I *am* created in God's image, that some aspect of me reflects some aspect of God that the world needs to see, that perhaps in charting my own course, I am helping others to find their own unique paths. And in prayer I have heard the words, "You are not alone; your pain is your strength."

No. I am not alone. When present-day rejections trigger memories of childhood, dredging up past pain, leaving me fragile and withdrawn, God reminds me of the ways in which I have been upheld, through it all. Over and over again, I see God's hand stretched out toward me in much the same way that a parent reaches out to a baby learning how to walk: the child totters toward the hand, straightens up, teeters over, then tries again, slowly gaining confidence and momentum. One of my earliest memories is of a winter walk along a gravel path near the sea. I am two or three years old, clutching my father's hand, trying, unsuccessfully, to keep up with his military stride. Suddenly, I break away—perhaps to investigate something we have passed by too quickly—and I fall. Tearfully, I examine my scraped hands and dirty leggings and scream, "You should've held my hand—I wouldn't have fallen down!" It is God's hand that has been consistently in mine, even in those times when I have felt most alone. It is God's hand that has never let go.... Even in those darkest moments when I reach for my guitar and pound out feelings of sadness that well up from the deepest part of self, I believe that God is there with me, listening to what strings and wood cry out....

# The Price of Higher Consciousness

Some of the most terrible words in the Christian scriptures are to be found in Matthew 10:

> "Do not suppose that I have come to bring peace to the earth: it is not peace I have come to bring but a sword. For I have come to set a man against his father, a daughter against her mother, a daughter-in-law against her mother-in-law. Your enemies will be those of your own household... Anyone who does not take up the cross and follow in my footsteps is not worthy of me." (Mt 10:34-39)

Jesus, in acknowledging himself as the source of dissension, challenges us to examine our own complacency, our own apathy, and our own contentment with the status quo. I have come to the conclusion that if we are really serious about the inner world, if we fully respond to the gospel message, then life can never be "predictable" again. Things we have taken for granted become strangely insignificant. Goals we have pursued no longer hold meaning. Relationships in which we have invested ourselves seem frivolous—or ashes! The more the gospel takes root in our hearts, the more we begin to change. Decisions about how we spend our time and money, where we worship, how we earn our living, what we eat and what we own are no longer arbitrary or habitual; rather, we make each choice in light of the truth of the gospel. In so doing, we may begin to separate ourselves from family and societal values.

The fullness of life to which Jesus invites us has its price. Few people settle for conscious living because it means constantly standing outside the circles of acceptability in which we formerly moved. As I have pursued heightened consciousness in my own life, I have experienced the paradox of becoming more at home with who I am yet increasingly "foreign" in terms of the culture. A "simple" trip to the grocery store can involve checking labels to see which companies might be subsidiaries of corporations whose products I boycott for humanitarian reasons—for selling baby formula to third world countries without making sterilizing procedures available, for example, or for producing armaments, or for unnecessarily cruel testing of cosmetics on animals, or for making a profit in countries presently under a trade embargo.... Similarly, one phone call from the peace and justice network can lead to writing letters to political representatives or to marching in Chicago's streets.... A job offer involves assessing how much time I will have for my inner life, rather than how much my income will increase.... And so it goes....

But there is a higher price to pay than minor inconveniences. After all, one can substitute Hershey's chocolate chips for Nestle's, Mobile oil for Shell, and peaches and plums for table grapes; and provided one doesn't get assaulted or arrested, participating in protest demonstrations is not usually hazardous—at least, not in the U.S., though there are, of course, other countries where one's very life is threatened for making political statements. No, the price I am referring to has to do with fractured relationships. By following one's own path, one can become "too much" for others who prefer to go on "living and partly living," and who may be filled with existential dread at the thought of anything which might interrupt life as they know it. In speaking the truth we experience in our own hearts, we threaten those with little tolerance for ambiguity or heightened emotions. Out of fear, family members, friends and colleagues may avoid us, mock us, put us down or behave in ways that are passive aggressive. Instead of hearing us, they hear, instead, their own projected fears, their own terror of having their narrow boundaries encroached upon. Our very presence can become a source of discomfort, a source of discord. By embracing the path of awareness, then, we also embrace the bitter cross of rejection.

I have touched on this reality both in workshops and in classes. When talking about the spiritual journey as a "hero quest," I often speak of the Road of Trials which ensues when we decide to follow the call of higher consciousness. So often, our growth in awareness leads to dramatic changes in attitude and behavior. These changes, for reasons stated above, can drive a wedge between friends, relatives and even spouses. The heroic response can be to leave things as they are or to move on, depending on the particular situation. Either way, as my students will attest, suffering follows. What is essential is that we steadfastly hold to the belief that nothing is more important than our spiritual journey; any choice we make needs to be determined in light of our relationship with God.

# God the Oyster

During intensely painful moments, the pain is sometimes more real than my experience of God. I feel it contorting my center, radiating through me until every bone, every muscle and every organ wants to scream out, "It hurts!" And the uncentered "I" loudly protests, "I can't stand it!" At such times, all that I know about surrender and letting go, about relaxation and "letting God," seems to disappear. I forget my repertoire of "helpful techniques" and, more foolishly, forget about asking God for help. Instead, my consciousness shrivels up, leaving me aware only of the situation at hand.

Disappointment and experiences of rejection can surface childhood memories, in spite of years of arduous inner work. Grief, then, is more than a present tense event, but reaches back into my earliest years, unscabbing wounds I believed had healed. Though I have faced core issues over and over again, though I have dared to name the hurts and to accept each one, yet there is a broken piece of my heart which seems to be beyond healing. Every time I return to Malta, I am made sharply aware of this. On the one hand, I feel drawn to go back—to "reconnect" with those who are dear to me, to walk once more near the Mediterranean, to enjoy Maltese cuisine, to drink in the beautiful scenery, to behold archeological and architectural gems which speak to my heart so deeply.... On the other hand, there is the price which each visit exacts—the reawakening of the reality of "not belonging," of being negated, of being expected to maintain the semblance of happiness in public and a code of silence regarding my true feelings.... Recently, as I was listening to the responsorial psalm during Sunday liturgy, the refrain triggered an uncontrollable fit of weeping. I don't remember the exact words but they had something to do with God healing the brokenhearted. My own heart promptly broke open with present tense grief and past tense grief. In the economy of my weeping, I mourned the pain of my life.

I felt embarrassed at this outburst. I was, after all, sitting in the front pew and a number of people around me were aware of my tears. I didn't want to have to explain "what was wrong"; any attempt to articulate the feelings which had overwhelmed me would set me off again, and I feared that once I started crying, I would not be able to stop. In my experience of fragility, I decided that I would *not* preach the following Sunday, and that I would take some time out from my free-lance work for my own healing.

As I reflected on this experience, the image came to me of an oyster—a pearl oyster, that is, rather than one of the edible kind. I know little about marine life, but one fact that has always fascinated me is the oyster's ability to transform an irritation—a grain of sand, for example—into an object of rare beauty. The mantle or fleshy organ which lines the inside of the shell secretes shell-forming substances around the irritation until a pearl is formed. What was of no worth, what was a source of aggravation, is now a treasure of great price.

If we are willing to allow God to reside at the circumference of our pain, then work of transformation *can* happen. God, like the oyster, can encircle our pain, not numbing us to it but allowing us to see its value. As I took this image to prayer, I understood that it was precisely because of unsatisfactory human relationships that I had turned to God as comforter, friend, lover.... The intensity of my love for God had, in large part, been born of my need for companionship, for nurturing. In God, I had found intimacy and unconditional love. Defining God as my primary relationship, then, was no mere lip service to an ideal: God was my lifeline in every sense. At the same time, I also came to understand that the passion and compassion I bring to ministry also have their source in this pain. Through God's grace, the hurts of four decades have become a pearl of great price. The challenge is for me to remember this.

# Being, Not Doing

Descartes may primarily be remembered for saying, "I think, therefore I am," but we who live at the edge of the third millennium will as surely be remembered for living out of a different reality: "I *do,* therefore I am." We are people who are constantly doing, who pride ourselves on our doing and who define ourselves by all that we accomplish. We are supermen and superwomen who have learned to balance jobs, family responsibilities, social obligations and leisure time with utmost efficiency—thanks to time-savers, five year calendars and technology. We schedule our exercise time and our leisure time, more to keep "the old machine running" than because we truly enjoy relaxing. We plan one activity after another, from prayer to bookkeeping, from quality family time to lovemaking.

Spontaneity is too inefficient for our whirlwind lives. When asked how we are, the refrain is so often, "too busy"—yet we are proud of our busyness, of our usefulness, of our productivity, of our importance. And so we rush from one meeting to the next, from one appointment to the next, from one task to the next. There is never enough time, it seems, for all that we have to accomplish. When we measure what we *have* actually done against what we *wished* we could have done, we are left dissatisfied. Because we see ourselves as cogs in an endlessly running machine, we push ourselves mercilessly, intent on achieving and producing more and still more.

For me, there has always been a tension between "doing" and "being," perhaps brought about by my need to prove myself in a world in which little was expected of me. In high school, for example, I was constantly juggling studies with being school captain, editing the yearbook, running the drama club, debating society and charity drive, participating in archeological digs— and all the while pursuing a rigorous academic program.... Part of me yearned "to be," to be free of all the anxiety and exhaustion that went hand in hand with such intense "doing," to have more time for relaxation and quiet; but part of me so delighted in these activities that I did not know how to sit still.

Today, my desire for contemplative space is much more acute, and yet necessity (and delight!) has created for me a unique position at DePaul University where, in addition to working with University Ministry as a spirituality resource/spiritual director, I also teach for three departments. Then there is my free-lance ministry which includes writing, preaching, spiritual direction, image guidance, retreats and workshops, as well as family responsibilities. Sometimes, all this gets to be "too much." All I want is to find some quiet hermitage (near the water's edge, of course) where I can write and pray.

Whereas before I thrived on variety and activity, now I suspect that it less healthy for me than I would like to believe. I have noticed that each time the school year begins, my system seems to go into shock. Until I get used to the work schedule again, I feel exhausted and get frequent headaches; I crave silence and solitude and literally have to force myself to be "public." Gradually, I am learning to say "no," both on campus and off campus. Gradually, I am learning to carve empty spaces into my life. Gradually, I am beginning to dream of a new way of being when free from the constraints of an intense schedule, I will be able to face tracts of "empty time" without lapsing into depression. Even as I write this, however, part of me recognizes the necessity for some activity in my life—for a healthy balance between the outer and inner worlds in which I move, for some involvement in the public sphere without my being "driven" to perform or to succeed. Ultimately, it is the extent to which I encounter God in all that I do—and in all that I do **not** do—that counts.... I need to learn to **be** in the doing....

# Broken Vessels

About seven years ago, my primary image of myself was of a pot—beautifully embellished, yes, but locked away in a cupboard so that it could neither be seen nor used. Aware of my gifts and desiring nothing more than to use them, I felt incredibly frustrated. I constantly asked God the potter to let me know my purpose in life. No answer seemed forthcoming.

Then, surprisingly, all kinds of opportunities broke open. Before long, I found myself with multiple ministries ranging from teaching to preaching, from university ministry to giving retreats, from running a ministry training program to writing books and articles on spirituality. Everything I did gave me great delight: I felt close to God and "useful." But the more useful I became, the more demands were made on my time. Invitations and requests came my way so rapidly that I felt overwhelmed. It was like being a child in a candy store, with a few dimes in her pocket and hundreds of possible choices. Like Tigger in *Winnie the Pooh* who had great difficulty in figuring out what Tiggers like for breakfast, I looked at my range of activities and no longer knew what I wanted to do with my life: I enjoyed everything I did; there was simply too much of it. The contemplative in me wanted to run....

Three years ago, I was not sure what the future would hold for me. A combination of a grueling schedule and painful stress within the family left me feeling fragile. Whereas in the past my enthusiasm and energy carried me through all kinds of public commitments, I began to feel I had little to give. It was as though all my innate gifts had been suspended, leaving me completely dependent on God to get me through. Each time I gave a class or presentation, it was God who organized my thoughts and gave me the insights to respond to students' questions. Each time I met with someone for spiritual direction, it was God who helped me to place my own issues behind me and to concentrate instead upon what was being said. Each time I proclaimed the word, it was God who moved through me, so that the word could be heard. I approached ministry from the perspective of one who had nothing to give but who trusted that God would use me, in spite of my present deficiencies.

Yes, I saw myself as a broken vessel—still able to contain the mystery of God, but with nothing to offer of my own. When people asked me how I was, I responded, "I'm in recovery," and meant it. At first, I thought a week of summer vacation would allow me to spring back to my former self, but this did not happen. Physically and emotionally, I was shattered....

In such times, the question which surfaces is, "What is God calling me to?" I don't believe that this kind of shattering happens for nothing; each time it happens, we are immersed in paschal mystery—in the nailing to the cross, in the descent into the darkness of the tomb, in the rising to new life in Christ. It is as though pain and weakness bring with them the opportunity to participate in the sufferings of Jesus, and in his vindication. For my part, I believe there is a valuable lesson in this dismemberment of self, that there may be a new call surfacing—one which very likely will entail leaving my former ways and attitudes behind me. One thing is clear: in the midst of pain and uncertainty, God is my joy and my strength; to the extent that Christ lives in me, so will God be able to use me in my brokenness.

# Spirit Embodied

In September 1993 I was a privileged participant in the Parliament of the World's Religions, in Chicago. Taking the opportunity to immerse myself more deeply in my own tradition, I also found myself enriched and expanded by the presence of Buddhists, Sikhs, Muslims, Sufis, Jews and countless other worshipers. I was left with a renewed sense of God's mystery and multi-facetedness, as well as with a heightened appreciation of diversity.

There were many memorable people with whom I came into contact during that week, but one stands out in particular. There was a fire in his eyes which seemed other-worldly; caught in his steady gaze, I felt an all-embracing love that left me both startled and peaceful. Later, a friend helped me understand this phenomenon: "He's like an angel," said my friend. "He has the most unusual eyes...."

In spite of the milling crowds, I again found myself sitting next to this angel during one of the major addresses. He held me with the same intense gaze and then, unexpectedly, put his hand on mine; and I, spontaneously, placed my right hand over his. As we listened to the presentation, I was aware of energy surging through me—his love, his peace. He was little more than a stranger, and yet I felt intimately connected to him, uniquely loved by him. And then, as surprisingly as we had met, he quietly stood up and left, before the presentation had even ended. I felt inexplicably bereft. I wanted to ask him, "What happened between us?"—but he was not there....

At first, I was perplexed by his leaving. Did he have an appointment? Was he himself giving a presentation? Was the intensity of our communion too much for him? (unlikely, I thought) Or was he concerned that it was too much for me? (quite possibly, I thought) Ironically, we had just been listening to Jean Houston's account of her chance meeting with Teilhard de Chardin, the amazing friendship that developed between the gawky teenager and the mysterious elderly gentleman, and her devastation at his later disappearance. In the space of a few moments, my experience had paralleled hers.

Later, as I reflected on this extraordinary interaction, the insight came to me that a mutual giving had taken place in our hand-holding. It was as though the spirit in each of us had seen itself reflected in the other. God reminded me that it was God's Spirit that brought us together, and that I need not feel abandoned. The spirit I had encountered was one and the same as the spirit which resided within me. God would not leave me orphaned....

My mind often wanders back to this burning encounter. I still experience a sense of loss, especially as it is unlikely that I will meet this angel again. But even as I regret not having had the chance for further conversation, for further gazing and hand-holding, I am energized by the desire to be like him: I, too, want to be a channel of God's healing love to others. The gift I received is the willingness to allow God such full residence within me that it is God—not I—who will be present to others. The call is to become nothing less than an angel—a messenger of God's love.

# Becoming Love

"Becoming love" comes from the direct experience of God's love and from the desire to share this love with others; it comes from the willingness to die to self so that God's love can be fully present. It is this reality that St. Paul writes about when he says, "There is only Christ: he is everything and he is in everything" (Col 3:11).

For longer than I would like to admit, I believed that loving others was a matter of will, of choosing to extend oneself. I thought that love came from the wellspring within, directly from our own goodness, from our own resources. Yes, we knew how to love because God had loved us first—that much I admitted—but I still regarded the ability to love as something innate, something we could "work on" and intensify, just as we could develop other skills and abilities.

In the last year or so, I have begun to see things differently. My understanding of what it means to be a Christian has changed dramatically, not as a result of laborious research or hours of private devotion, but as a result of a new awareness of Christ's presence—an intrusive presence at times, which constantly and insistently invites me to pay greater attention to the Christ-life within. Though I have always loved the liturgy and the gospels, my own prayer life has been more God-centered than Christic. Now, the reverse has happened: when I am drawn to pray, away from my own agenda (a common experience for me), it is the

41

presence of Jesus which beckons; when I pray, it is the second person of the Trinity who is present to me.

More and more, this Christ-presence is defining my spirituality—my piety, if you will. Whereas I used to interpret the many dark nights of my experience as occasions for my own transformation into a freer, more loving and more compassionate human being, I now understand that a deeper transformation is required. To say that I am pursuing wholeness or complete individuation is not enough: the language which suggests itself is that my own process of conversion will only be complete when I have allowed Christ to reside in me so fully that it is *his* presence, *his* love and *his* power that others encounter in my presence.

My old attitude toward the inner journey was probably not that different than most people's. I could measure my progress through tools of psychological evaluation, felt improvement and others' affirmation; I could use the traditional stages of the mystical journey to understand how I had moved from darkness, through illumination, to intense moments of union. Suddenly, however, definitions broke down, and I realized there was more dying to be done. I could no longer view myself as a work of art in progress, with myself as the primary subject; rather, I was the roughly hewn rock which had to be completely chipped away before the real self—the Christ self—could shine through.

What this means in terms of loving is that my real task is to surrender to that inner presence which is Love Incarnate. Instead of hoping that those I encounter experience me as a com-passionate person, I hope instead that they experience Christ's compassionate presence through me. Instead of hoping that those with whom I work recognize my skills as a healer of the spirit, I hope instead that they experience the skills of Christ the healer. Instead of hoping that others find motivation and energy through *my* charisma, through *my* creativity, I hope insteadthat they see beyond my gifts, to the presence of the indwelling God. To become Love, then, is nothing less than to allow Christ to reside at the center of self.

# Spiritual Intimacy

Recently, several women have shared with me stories of romances which unexpectedly made a difference in their lives. Each of them is at a stage in life when falling in love seems like an improbability: one, recently widowed, is in her mid-eighties; the other two have been divorced for so long that their main preoccupation until recently has been financial survival. For all three, romantic involvement has brought new energy, new hopefulness, and, perhaps most importantly, a new perception of self. Careworn creases have disappeared from their faces; instead, there is a look of youthfulness, tenderness and contentment. Each is surprised at the mystery that has touched them .

As I reflect on my friends' stories, I am struck by the new meaning each has found in her special relationship: they no longer feel "alone," or "misunderstood," or "unloved." These gifts are ones that each of us craves for, whether or not there is a romantic relationship in our lives. Sometimes, we find company, understanding and acceptance in the presence of spouse or "significant other"; more rarely, we find them through spiritual friendship.

Though spiritual friendship often includes the relationship between a spiritual director and directee, it is not limited to this model of relating. In my own life, spiritual intimacy has been an amazing grace which I have shared with several friends, as well as with two cherished spiritual directors, a skilled therapist and a minister whom I see for supervision in my own work of formation and spiritual companioning. It is not that I discount the romantic—I would not be married if this were the case—but there is a depth to human experience which can go deeper still, and which needs articulation, affirmation and nurturing.

Spiritual intimacy has allowed me to explore my experience of God with those who are also committed to this work of discovery. In some cases, there has been a ready "give and take," a mutual sharing which has led to extraordinary friendship. What brings self and other together is nothing less than the desire to speak about the mystery of God's action in our lives, to savor that mystery, to take joy in the other's joy, to be an understanding presence for the other, to reflect back all that one has seen and heard. In other cases, there have been "professional boundaries," so that the relationship is less equal but no less enriching. Here, the focus has been on *my* encounter with God, on *my* relationship with God, on the way God approaches *me*. The gift I receive from the other's undivided attention is the ability to focus exclusively on my spiritual journey; however, though the mentor in this situation may share little of self during our time together, the way he or she "sits" with me, the presence reflected in word and gesture, the felt compassion and heart-spoken prayer all create a sense of "inner connectedness" which transcends knowing the details of the other's life. Spiritual intimacy, then, is possible, even if we don't know the other in more traditional ways.

For me, the gift of spiritual intimacy is what keeps me faithful to my journey, even in those times when God seems inaccessible. Transcending frequency of contact and geographical distance, this intimacy is a wellspring of joy and courage. Often, the mere remembering of someone with whom I am spiritually connected brings with it peace, gratitude and delight. In the remembering, I rediscover my higher self and find, mirrored back to me, a reflection of God's love.

# Spending Time with God

Over the last few days, I have been aware of how little time there has been for God. There have been fewer gaps in my schedule; the days have begun earlier and ended later, but classes, meetings and appointments have run into each other with little breathing space in between. In addition, we are in the midst of selling our house and packing up our belongings to move to a new home. This not only requires physical energy, but there are all the stresses involved with dealing with real estate agents, potential buyers, mortgage representatives and lawyers. Acting on a growing impulse, today I stopped at the Fullerton Cenacle on the way to campus, hoping to spend some time in the chapel. To my relief, the sister on duty had no problems with my request and, in fact, personally escorted me to the upper room where the Blessed Sacrament is permanently exposed.

As I made myself comfortable on the floor, propped up by cushions, I realized the sense of loss I experience when there isn't time to pray. It is not that I am nagged by guilt for not stretching an impossible schedule, but I experience what I can only describe as "deprivation"—the absence of what gives my life meaning. I do experience God's presence in my teaching and ministry, but it is the quality of this presence—its intensity—which I miss.

I pondered over why it was that I felt drawn to the upper room. Both at work and at home, my office has increasingly become a place of accessibility where I can be reached via phone, a knock on the door, or by a mail delivery; and there are always memos to attend to, or papers to grade or presentations to plan. Moreover, my "sacred space" at home is now filled with stacks of books and empty boxes; though I have left art work on the walls so that I am still surrounded by icons which can draw me into mystery, it very much feels as though my prayer environment has already been dismantled. But it was more than a "safe" place for which I was looking: the presence of the Sacrament was the definite draw. My theology of Eucharist and my actual piety are in conflict here. I believe that the Eucharist belongs in the community, to be broken and shared with God's people so that we, too, can become bread for the world. Eucharist, then, is action, not an object. Intellectually, part of me says that the exposing of consecrated bread for private devotion "thingifies" eucharist—in fact, the monstrance seems to imprison the wafer, to fossilize it. I find myself wondering how often the consecrated wafer is "changed," if at all. But there is the traditional Catholic in me that delights in the symbolic: to have a tangible sense of the sacred gives me a sense of belonging, an experience of warmth....

Closing my eyes, I tried to focus on the presence of Christ. Though there are always a torrent of needs to present, I decided that this time I would provide God with the silence to speak to me. Since I had not done much listening of late, I thought God might want to use the time to let me know of anything to which I needed to pay attention—perhaps there were changes in lifestyle or attitudes that I needed to consider, or possibly I needed to reconsider aspects of my ministry. As I practiced the art of silence, I was aware of myriad colorful images, of a cast of intangible characters, of words and phrases that jolted through my consciousness. Every now and again, I would catch myself drifting in to sleep, and I would jolt myself back to concentration until the whole process began again. A predominant image which surfaced frequently was that of a pile of oriental rugs which a merchant was displaying for my benefit. Coincidentally, I had made a brief detour to Sahara Rugs before stopping at the

Cenacle: I had my heart set on an oriental rug for the new house, but though the store had slashed prices drastically, the rugs which appealed to me cost thousands of dollars and those I *could* afford would not have worked in the setting I envisioned. The rug issue had become something of an obsession, and so it was not surprising that images of hand-knotted rugs from Iran, Pakistan and Turkey splashed hues of orange and red across the palette of my mind.

Each time I tried to dismiss the troublesome rugs, new images would surface. I found myself growing irritated. "Here I am, God," I said. "I've gone out of my way to come here so that we could spend some time together, and nothing is happening except these images. I've given you the time to communicate with me and I can't even keep awake...." After nearly two hours of fruitless effort, I rose to my feet, stiff from all the sitting, and left.

It was in the short drive between the Cenacle and DePaul that understanding came. "Do you think that my communicating with you is limited to your putting aside a few hours for the purpose?" God seemed to say. "Don't you realize that I can speak to you through all the events of your life—even the rugs?" Humbled, I realized that the quest for a new rug when our budget was already stretched beyond what was prudent represented a kind of willfulness on my part; humbled, I recognized that by allotting God a couple of hours here and there for the express purpose of communicating with me, I had been trying to control not only how prayer "happened" but also our relationship. Conversation with God could not be conveniently compartmentalized, but needed to be constant, ongoing and spontaneous, regardless of my schedule and other distractions in my life.

# Deeper Loving

"I know that a deeper purging is necessary to take me to deeper levels of loving—and I am afraid of the pain." I remember this statement well, coming as it did during our Lenten reconciliation service; days earlier, during a rigorous session with my supervisor in ministry, I had come to the realization that I was avoiding prayer because I was resisting further growth. At the time, I had prayed a prayer of acceptance, inviting God to transform me in any ways which were necessary; it was this new willingness that I chose to ritualize during reconciliation. My hope was that by verbalizing my sin of fear, I would find the courage for whatever lay ahead.

The "purging" happened the next day, swiftly and dramatically—at least, that was my perspective. To the casual bystander, nothing out of the ordinary took place. The scene went something like this: student constantly called faculty member at home; faculty member felt harassed and expressed indignation to a few colleagues; student overheard; there were a few awkward moments but no real damage was done. My experience of the situation, however, was very different.

The student—I will call him Joe—had taken two of my classes and a workshop several years before. I was one of the first professors he had encountered at DePaul, and he made no secret of his regard for me. Three years later, when he approached me about writing a letter of recommendation to help him get into graduate school, I was more than happy to oblige. There began my difficulties. Over a period of several weeks, Joe began phoning me at home, at all hours—first to tell me that he was going to drop off the forms I needed to fill out, then to explain that he hadn't dropped them off after all, then to ask me to review his letter of application, then to question me about the revisions I suggested, then…and then…and then…. Finally, after receiving a phone call at 7:30 a.m., I told him, very irritably, to stop calling me at home. I drove in to school feeling frustrated and angry, and had barely set foot in the Religious Studies Department when the secretary told me that Joe had already been asking for me. At this point, I thrust an envelope containing Joe's revised revisions of his application statement into her hands and said, "I'm tired of being harassed. If he comes in again, I'M NOT HERE—I don't want to see him again!" Something in Beth's expression made me spin around. There, barely three or four feet behind me, stood Joe, face bright red. "That's me," he said, referring, I presume, to my description of the troublesome student; "that's mine," he continued, reaching out for the envelope which was already in Beth's hands. He thanked me graciously for my help, and, without commenting on what he had overhead, walked out of the department.

In that moment, I felt the world spinning beneath my feet. Incapable of moving, I found myself losing my equilibrium as the room spun faster. The blood rushed to my head, and for a few seconds I thought I was going to faint. Somebody tried to reassure me that he couldn't have heard what I had said, but I knew that he had. As I clutched a desk for support, I knew precisely how devastated Joe must have felt—how rejected, how disillusioned, how betrayed. Yes, he *had* invaded my privacy and, yes, he *had* pushed me beyond patience, but his grip on life was tentative and, as "the adult in charge," I should have known better than to express my feelings in a place where I could be overhead. And apart from writing him an awkward note of apology, there was nothing I could do to "fix" the situation.

All that day, I carried with me the knowledge of how deeply I had hurt Joe. I was surprised at the intensity of the pain I felt, especially when I could concentrate on nothing else. Never have I been more in touch with my own capacity to hurt others or my own need for forgiveness. The next day, Holy Thursday, as I spent time in the parish prayer chapel after the evening liturgy, I found myself identifying Joe's pain with Jesus' agony. It was as though Gethsemane had become a present tense reality. On an experiential level, what had become real for me was my place among the characters responsible for Christ's passion: my failure to love Joe was simultaneously—and mysteriously—the failure to love the God of love. On a logical level, of course, none of this makes much sense. Given the way Joe overstepped boundaries, my outburst was at least understandable. My experience of what happened, however, became a source of deep, soul-troubling grief which I could not let go until the veneration of the cross on Good Friday. I moved into Easter with a new humility, a stronger sense of accountability and—I hope—a deeper capacity for loving.

# Accepting God's Gifts

I have a tendency to assume that growth primarily happens through the process of suffering. A memorable refrain in Aeschylus' trilogy, *The Oresteia*, is, "we suffer into truth" and I believe that much of my own truth has come in this fashion. The ongoing cycle of light and darkness which has been so much a part of my experience has led me to heights and depths for which I am grateful, even if I would have rather done without the suffering. To find wholeness without suffering would be gift indeed, but I am not naive enough to assume that this is possible.

At the same time, I have just begun to grasp the fact that my own imagination is sadly limited when it comes to understanding God's ways of working. While most growth seems to involve suffering of one kind or another, it also seems that growth can happen in times of abundance. Over the last few months, life has been extraordinarily rich. There have been opportunities for extensive travel, for teaching in new programs, for attending conferences, for publishing my work; there have been friends to stay from out of state and relatives from overseas; and now there is the new house—close to the heart of the city, to our parish, St. James, and to work. As a friend commented before returning to France, "you have a very nice life."

Yes, I have to admit that I live very comfortably. There is endless variety to my ministry, and there are endless opportunities for my own inner work—for meaningful connections

with people who are serious about their spirituality. My
environment is aesthetically beautiful, and while I could always
name a few wants, there is nothing I desperately need. My
husband, Jim, and I are moving into a new stage of living in
which there is time for leisure (sadly missing before) and fewer
stresses such as hours of commuting and extensive yard work;
even our teenagers are beginning to settle down. I am very
conscious of God's bounty at this time in my life and feel quite
overwhelmed at the good things which have come my way.

These days, I am experiencing a new calmness of spirit, a
slowing down, an ongoing state of serenity. Classes are over for
the summer and I am looking forward to two months of
swimming, writing, lakeside relaxation and family reunions
spanning three continents. Part of me wonders if this can last; part
of me fears that the "darkness-light-darkness" cycle will resume;
part of me asks why I should have such a "nice life" when others
are engaged in so much struggling. With the memory of my own
struggles still such a part of my consciousness, I fear the
cessation of calm.

But while my shadow side may have difficulty in believing
that one can consistently enjoy life, my "redeemed side"
recognizes God's gifts and is grateful. Through my delight in a
new home and in a less hectic schedule, I feel increasingly
"whole," far less fragmented than in the days of two to three hour
commutes in heavy traffic—and far healthier than in the
emotionally shattering days of "acting out teenagers." I welcome
this lull in the storm of life and am aware of the renewal that is
happening in the deepest layers of self—renewal which is
essential for the ongoing effectiveness of my ministry and for my
own sense of hopefulness.

Hope, I have decided, is as necessary as compassion when one
is working with those who are suffering. If I cannot listen to
another's pain and help that person to connect with a sense of
ultimate meaning (which in itself is always ultimately hopeful),
then I have simply provided a temporary bandaid, not a tool to

live by. And if I myself fail to live out of hopefulness, then I am too personally impoverished to be in the business of helping others with their own spiritual issues. For as long as this unexpected phase of abundance is part of my reality, I will therefore try to savor it to the fullest extent possible—not because it may be of short duration (which well may be the case), but because God is using this time for my healing and renewal.

# Highest Power

The language of twelve-step programs allows those struggling with addictions or those continuing the ongoing work of recovery to acknowledge a power higher than themselves. Even if they are uncomfortable naming or believing in God, members of AA, OA and other such groups need to admit to themselves that there is "something" of greater ultimate meaning than their own agendas, desires or habits. Without this recognition of a "higher power," it is difficult to maintain a sense of commitment to the healing process or a sense of accountability; at the same time, the absence of this recognition leads one to assume that he or she is "in charge," whereas it is only through abandoning oneself completely and utterly to "ultimate meaning" that one can move beyond addiction.

This basic truth is applicable to all who journey on the spiritual path: unless God is our "highest power" in truth as well as in word, then we will not get very far. The problem is that very often, we invest ultimate power in institutions or in individuals, allowing them to govern our decisions and actions, rather than God; and, sad to say, we are not even aware that we are doing this. In fact, we might even assume that we are "doing God's will" by listening to these external voices of authority.

Today, as I was reading *The National Catholic Reporter*, I found myself becoming increasingly saddened by Pope John Paul II's statement in his apostolic letter, *Ordinatio Sacerdotalis*, May

30, 1994: "I declare that the church has no authority whatsoever to confer priestly ordination on women and that this judgment is to be definitively held by all the church's faithful." The statement not only continues the prohibition against the ordination of women for the Catholic priesthood, but also bans Catholics from supporting women's ordination—presumably, in thought, word or deed. I am left wondering what women like myself—women, that is, who feel called to the priesthood—are to do when there is a fundamental discrepancy between God's invitation and the church's hierarchical response.

The deep pain that comes from the desire to use my gifts as fully as possible in the service of Christ's church is not something I can easily dismiss. One Sunday, about twelve years ago, my proclamation of the Word had a powerful impact on both the presider and the assembly; following the liturgy, the priest, a visitor to our parish, asked me, "If you could choose to do anything with your life, what would you do?" "I would be ordained," I said, then promptly wept. And since that time, my lay status has been an open wound which deepens as I discover more and more ministerial gifts within myself.

To the extent possible, I have claimed my baptismal legacy of priesthood. Through national involvements and home parish ministry, I have used and been affirmed in my gifts, yet this has not been enough to lessen the sting of loss. It is not that I desire to wear a Roman collar (the pink teddy bear in my office does that) or to be installed in some pristine rectory, or, for that matter, to be called "Reverend" and be part of the vested club. No, it is simpler than this. It really amounts to bread and wine, to oil and water, to ritual gestures and sacred words. It amounts to taking bread into my hands and saying, "This is my body which will be given up for you"; it amounts to taking the cup and saying, "This is the cup of my blood, the cup of the new and everlasting covenant...." It involves rituals of initiation and rituals of healing; it involves walking with God's holy people from birth to burial as friend and guide, as comforter....

This wound I suffer would not magically disappear with the rite of ordination. Over the years, enough hands have been laid upon me to make me feel fully called and fully anointed by those I have served. For it is not the absence of the ordination rite but the absence of the office of priest, particularly in its sacramental character, that causes me pain: it is my heart's desire to serve as the spiritual leader of a worshiping community, to mediate the presence of Jesus through administering the sacraments.

In the course of this time, I have prepared others—both Catholic men and Protestant men and women—for ordination, knowing full well that I was just as prepared as they to become a "person of the cloth." What do I say to the "Highest Power" who has instilled this desire in me? According to the pope, this very desire is willful, disobedient and clearly out of line. And what do I say to my students who ask me why I still remain Catholic when I speak so passionately about women's ordination?

Ultimately, over this as well as over every other issue, it is to God I must finally answer, not to the Vatican. I believe that God is the source of both my gifts and of my desires and that God is calling me—as well as countless other women—into priestly service. This implies, of course, that the prohibition against women's ordination is contrary to God's will and that it represents resistance to the action of the Holy Spirit. To the extent that I can continue using my priestly gifts **within** the church, I believe I am responding to God's call in a way that sets a course for other women who **will** one day be ordained to the Catholic priesthood. If, however, I find myself silenced, thwarted and censored, then it will be time to abandon my vocation into God's hands—where it rightly belongs anyway—and to see whether my "call" will take me on a different journey from the one I had envisioned.

# Servanthood

I am always moved when my spiritual director prays for me and with me at the end of a session or during sacramental reconciliation. Though the content of the praying is as varied as the material I present, yet there is one consistent element: Tom always refers to me as, "Liz, your servant," and each time I hear these words, I am touched to the core. I have not yet explored this reaction with Tom—perhaps because I don't want to make him self-conscious in his praying. The words about servanthood flow from him naturally and I receive them as gift—as compliment, perhaps. Each time I hear the phrase, I experience a sense of awe that I am somehow participating in advancing God's reign, in extending the ministry of Jesus. I feel Tom's affirmation of what I do—a recognition that while I cannot be ordained, yet I am living out my baptismal commitment to priestly ministry. Poignancy and gratitude co-exist as I remember the call to "be Christ" for others....

It is somehow ironic that a word like "servanthood" should move me so deeply. I grew up with servants in a culture which classified people into two basic groups: those whose birthright was to be served and those whose station in life was to serve them. As a child, I took for granted the fact that, six days a week, the maid arrived at our house before 7:00 a.m. and did not leave until 6:00 p.m. I even resented her Sunday absence, for this meant that my sisters and I would have to help out with setting the table and washing dishes after meals—the only chores expected of us. It did not dawn on me that she had a life outside our home, or that she might look forward to days off. Then there was Carmel, my father's batman (a soldier assigned to serve military officers), whose function in life was to press my father's uniforms, polish all our shoes, clean the brass and do odd jobs around the house, and Angelo, the gardener, whose feet were as dark and cracked as the dry earth.... According to the mindset of the privileged, servants were "nobodies"—barely human, in fact. They were to be treated kindly but firmly, and, at all times, without excessive familiarity; there was never to be any confusion as to who was serving whom, for the whole class system depended on maintaining clear boundaries.

Coming from such a society, I suppose it is surprising that the word "servant" should have positive connotations for me of any kind. On the contrary, far from finding it demeaning, I consider it empowering. To be servant means to be "useful," something I did not feel growing up. Just as the culture defined servants by menial work, so the culture also defined women's status by their lack of employment, by their leisurely lifestyle. To be female was to be dependent on male relatives for security; to be female was to settle for life as an accessory. What heightened this sense of uselessness for me was my own scholastic inability in terms of any work which we would now deem "left-brained." I could not do math, in spite of hours of drilling; I could not parse sentences in English or analyze metric form in poetry; I could not remember the underlying grammatical rules for French or Latin, let alone Maltese. On the other hand, I excelled in creative writing, literature, history, art, classical culture, drama, singing.... These, accomplishments, however, did little to raise my self-esteem or to help me imagine that college would ever be an option. By the time I was fifteen, I no longer believed that the future held any possibility for me, other than to be "somebody's wife" and bored. It was only when I had the good fortune to have a renaissance woman from the north of England as a teacher that I developed a passion for learning and realized that I was not so useless, after all.

To be servant also means to be "needed." During my growing up years, we certainly needed our servants to run the household; they had the inexhaustible energy necessary for the upkeep of a large home, and by performing their jobs well, they freed my sisters and me from having to take time away from studies or relaxation. Yes, we were spoiled, and, yes, we rapidly had to learn domesticate skills when we got married, but childhood was certainly a time of indulgence: nobody really needed us to *do* anything or *be* anything, or so it would seem. Now, I often feel overwhelmed at how many people seem to need (or want) my skills; I feel fully employed, at times overextended, but grateful for my usefulness in God's scheme of things. It is in my servanthood that I feel most fully alive, most fully human, and most fully in touch with what it means to be an icon of God's grace....

And yet—there is always a yet—I have to come back to that simple word, "being." In spite of my delight in active servant-hood, I do believe that it is in **being** that we most fully serve God. Last Lent, my parish invited parishioners to an experience of prayer partnership. We would meet three times at the church for a communal prayer service, but would have time for sharing with our partners built into the experience. To my disappointment, my partner was unable to leave her apartment, owing to infirmity. I decided to attend opening prayer at St. James and then spend a little time at Marjorie's home.

Marjorie—an African American who has just turned eighty-nine—has taught me that one can actively "be" while "doing" little. A "Minister of Praise," she holds the needs of the world in her heart and spends much of her time praying for special intentions. After I listened to her concerns, I shared with her those things I had brought with me—things I had never expected to share with a prayer partner. She listened quietly, sympathetically, and I felt a surge of emotion at the thought of her holding me in her prayers through the days ahead. As I left, she asked me if I had any family—meaning parents and siblings. When I explained that they were in Europe and South Africa, she said, "I'll be your family." I could barely hold back the tears....

# Keeping Chaos from the Center

Two years ago, my dream imagery was unsettlingly predictable. Night after night, I would dream of green churning waters which threatened to overwhelm both me and my family. Typically, I would be driving down an expressway, my husband and children as passengers, when the road would become virtually impassable. Or we would be driving down a sheer cliff and again the flood waters would rise, threatening to sweep us off the path, onto the treacherous rocks waiting below. The most dramatic dream was when the flood waters threatened to break through every window of our house. While Jim and the children retreated upstairs, I saw myself pushing closed all the shutters in a desperate attempt to save us from destruction. The image of my outstretched hands pressing against the shutters remains with me to this day: both in dreaming and waking, I knew we were on a dangerous path and that it was my task to protect the family.

To go into the details of mid-life crises and adolescent rebellion is unnecessary here. It just so happened that, as in many other families, chaos erupted in full force, seemingly without specific cause but with traumatic effects for all of us. It seemed that we were constantly dealing with major crises; hardly a weekend went by without some stressful incident, and it reached a point where I was grateful to go to work, since that was the only place of calm. Home had become a hostile environment.

Today, when I remember those events of not so long ago, I am still filled with wonder that, in the first place, "we made it," and, secondly, that I was able to carry on with my busy schedule and still function effectively. There is no doubt in my mind that it was God who carried me through this turmoil, or that it was God who was my strength, my inspiration, my creativity. I was exhausted, demoralized, and profoundly sad, and yet each time I got up to give a class, each time I preached or gave a retreat, each time I had someone alone with me in my office for spiritual direction or crisis work of some kind, I was able to forget my own concerns and to be present to the needs of the moment. Even as my domestic world threatened to disintegrate, I continued publishing my work and giving public presentations. In spite of the grieving, I was at peace.

I am no stranger to discord, but this experience of serenity in the heart of chaos *was* something new to me. In the past, I would have most likely become physically ill as a result of all the stress and would have certainly been preoccupied with agonizing over what could not be changed or with finding "quick fixes" for each situation. Something in me had obviously "shifted," and this shift was the work of grace.

It was grace, I believe, which kept me faithful to prayer when it would have been easier to have spent my energy in anger or anxiety. It was grace which gifted me with such an overwhelming sense of the presence of God that my family situation faded in importance. It was grace that awakened the spirit of enthusiasm, the spirit of compassion and the spirit of wonder so that I could perceive meaning beyond chaos. In former times, I would have played "martyr" (or victim), wallowing in self-pity and boring my friends with complaints. Now, I discovered, by fixing my gaze upon the face of the risen Christ, I no longer had to define myself by my suffering. The pain was merely something I was going through—hard and dreadful, yes, but only one aspect of the reality in which I found myself. Pain is passing, I discovered; it is not ultimate. When we regard chaos as the whole truth about ourselves and the world in which we live, then we dishonor the presence of God in our midst. When, however, we recognize God's action within the whirlwind itself, then we know beyond all knowing that God is with us and for us, no matter how terrible the storm....

# Spiritual Tools

Among photographs of Maltese temples and gothic cathedrals, a rather unusual photograph hangs on one of the walls in my DePaul office on the Lincoln Park campus. At first glance, one is struck by the intensity of the green among all the depictions of white stone. Then, as one is drawn more closely into the subject matter, other details begin to surface: the heads of several mannequins impaled on poles among lush vegetation in a waterway, and an ominous sign which states, in faded letters, "Welcome—if you have webbed feet." I had snapped this shot while out on a boat with some friends in Florida and had been struck by the strange juxtaposition of words and images.

It was only later that I begin to reflect on some the implications of this scenario. The spiritual journey is very much like an adventure into deep waters, and if one is not equipped with "webbed feet," it can be perilous. For me, having "webbed feet" means knowing one's strengths and limitations, being aware of the past without being "stuck" in it, having a guide as "helper" along the way, taking time out for prayer and leisure, having a healthy acceptance of self, and, most importantly, constantly paying attention to where God might be leading. It means having holy flexibility, healthy detachment, deep compassion for all living things and an authentic enthusiasm for life; it means being in balance.

Without "webbed feet," we place ourselves and others at

existential risk. The spiritual journey can become a ruthless quest in which "perfection," "forgetfulness," or "transcendental experience" is the goal, rather than the desire to please God. When we seek to numb memory or desire through religious experience, or to prove self-worth, or to have constant "highs," then the journey becomes self-serving rather than God-serving and is both its own end and its own reward.

At the same time, if we ignore the work of healing that each of us needs to do and, instead, forge ahead without paying attention to the wounds of our experience, then the shadow can surface precisely when we imagine we are most invincible—and it can wreak havoc. For Carl Jung, the shadow is that dimension of the self created by what has not yet come to light, either through unconscious repression or through deliberate forgetting. When we are courageous enough to do our shadow work, then we slowly but methodically bring to the surface that which needs to be made manifest. This is hard but empowering work which ultimately leads us to greater consciousness; however, when for one reason or another we fail to do this work, the shadow can become demonic in its fury and can undermine life as we know it.

The irony is that the more intensely we journey spiritually, the more imperative it is for us to do our "shadow work." Our capacity for light, it seems, is matched by our capacity for darkness. When we forget this reality and carry on as though evil does not exist, then we can unleash terrible forces, both in us and around us: for if we fail to recognize our shadow, then not only are *we* likely to "act out" in surprising ways or find ourselves in crisis, but those closest to us—whether family or friends or colleagues—may also begin to live out of this shadow. It is neither coincidence nor mere hearsay that those involved in healing work often experience acute difficulties within their own families, or else have to deal with agonizing personal struggles.

My understanding of just how essential it is to have "webbed feet" was brought home to me through a childhood friend's suicide. Though our ways had parted with our growing up, we had stayed connected, perhaps because we shared the same birthday, the winter solstice. I remember reflecting on the significance of this day in one of my occasional letters to David; the theme of light in darkness gripped us both, as did the mythical significance of this shortest of days. I could make no sense of this death, coming as it did after my friend had begun to turn his life around. Having dropped out of boarding school at sixteen, he had finally found happiness in his late thirties—a new wife, world travel and the discovery of Buddhism as a way to personal truth.

Later correspondence with his wife finally surfaced some clues. David had begun meditating on a regular basis, sometimes for three or four hours at a stretch; at first, he experienced greater peacefulness as a result of meditating, but then he began to hear voices—voices which told him that he had killed someone in a former life and that he therefore had to kill himself to atone for what he had done. Believing he was hearing the voice of God, David obeyed.

The pieces suddenly made sense. I remembered details of David's childhood—his mother's death from cancer when he was barely three, his father's constant harping that David was responsible for his mother's death, the beatings he received from the aunt who raised him and from the monks at the boarding school he attended, adolescent trouble with the law.... The voices he had heard were none other than his father's voice of accusation. Buried deep within David's unconscious was the notion that he had murdered his mother (she had developed cancer while she was pregnant with him); because he had never dealt with this conviction, the voice had taken on a demonic life of its own, becoming, as he thought, "the voice of God." In taking his own life, David performed the supreme act of obedience, but unlike Abraham, there was no guardian angel to stay his hand....

To embark upon long hours of prayer or meditation without a guide and without having done the foundational work of inner healing, then, allows the shadow to surface in seemingly divine form, even though, in reality, it can be demonic. The healing of past wounds must always precede or accompany descending deeply into the spiritual realm; this is not work we can usually accomplish alone.

# Locked Doors

A number of years ago, I was in the painful situation of being in a parish whose pastor, rather than welcoming my gifts, felt threatened by them—or by me, perhaps. Whatever the case, the impact was the same: my skills were not needed. As a brand new "Doctor of Ministry" who had just completed an internship in spiritual direction and who was ready to minister within that parish, I was devastated. Even my dreams began to reflect my sense of hopelessness. I remember one dream in particular in which I was standing at the bottom of the church steps, looking up at my pastor; vested in green, he was standing in front of the church doors, arms folded across his chest, face set grimly. The doors themselves were painted a glossy black and were firmly shut. I don't recall any movement in the dream, but these images evoked for me the pain of the situation—and also its absurdity. It would seem that given the multiple demands facing the church today and given the limited nature of resources, any parish would welcome the contributions of someone who has both the training and the willingness to serve. In effect, I felt silenced and discounted—not by the people, but certainly by the pastor; worse still, I had to deal with his misinterpretations of my motives for wanting to serve in the first place. This was treatment I had not anticipated, but further reflection makes me wonder how many women have similar stories to tell about the way they have fared within their own parishes. To have one's desire to minister dismissed as "wanting to be in the limelight" or, worse still, as "sexual pursuit" is not a situation to be brushed off lightly....

The locked doors of my dream became a powerful symbol of the forces which can temporarily limit the work of the Holy Spirit. As I sat in my pew, Sunday after Sunday, as I spent hours pondering whether or not I should look for another parish, I never anticipated the power of the Spirit to break through those same doors. In my pain, in my sense of being thwarted, in my confusion, I lost sight of my options; I *hoped* that things would change, but could not believe that they really would. To experience God's call and then to see opportunities to respond to that call disappear was disorienting.

It was about this time that Mundelein College closed its doors—not only to me, but to all the students, faculty and staff who had loved it so deeply. I had served as adjunct faculty in Graduate Religious Studies for a period of about six years and had set my hopes on a full-time teaching position there. To be working in spirituality at the depth possible with adult students who were mostly religious professionals was incredibly life-giving. I found myself renewed by each classroom experience, and each course functioned as an extended retreat for me and for my students. When I learned that Loyola was to acquire Mundelein College and that only a select few of the tenured faculty would be retained, I felt as though everything I had worked toward had suddenly disintegrated. I *did* have other opportunities for ministry, but Mundelein was where my heart was.

But though I constantly fall into the same old heresy of "deadendedness," that is, of disbelief in the future, things changed. I was so preoccupied in grieving over lost opportunities that I failed to notice the new things which were coming my way. At DePaul University where I was coming to the end of my contract as a full-time English instructor, I was able to negotiate a joint appointment with English and University Ministry. This transition—which eventually became a joint appointment with Religious Studies and University Ministry—not only made use of my existing skills, but also strengthened my abilities as retreat leader, counselor, preacher and leader of prayer. My most popular course at Mundelein—"Myths, Signs and Symbols"—transferred into DePaul's School for New Learning where I was again working with adult students, this time mostly from the business world. Soon, I was not only offering spiritual direction on campus and in a free-lance capacity, but I also began an archdiocesan-sponsored training program for spiritual companions to serve in a parish setting.

What I have learned from all of this is that there is no telling which way the Spirit will blow, nor what call will manifest itself at a particular time. Looking back, I realize that in some ways my dreams were too small. Had I been allowed to minister in my former parish, I probably would have focused all my energies there, even in a volunteer capacity, rather than look for a more public arena. Had Mundelein remained open, I would have continued to "preach to the converted," rather than evangelize in the desert where my work so often takes me. It would seem that those involved in ministry need, above all else, to trust that the One who called them will indeed find a place for their gifts—not because they have a *right* to these gifts, but because God's work needs to be done.

# Lord of Time

As I write this, we have now lived in our new home for about a month. Treasured art work, plants and books are in place, and the house—particularly my study where I pray, write and meet with people for spiritual direction—is becoming sacred space. In the first days after we moved, before the mini blinds were up and while there were still construction workers on the roof and, seemingly, in every window, I felt disoriented—completely unable to pray. I had functioned as an automaton for several weeks in that frantic time of packing, selling the old house, working on campus, traveling extensively and keeping up with freelance commitments. Now that I was ready to slow down and simply "be," I neither felt at home with myself nor with the house. That has changed.

For the first time since I can remember, I am enjoying life. I don't mean to imply that I have never enjoyed life; on the contrary, I have an extraordinary capacity for living, but there has been so much stress over the last few years that, while there were isolated moments of pure joy, most of my energy has gone into surviving. Yes, I took time out to be with friends, to swim on a regular basis and to work in the garden; and, yes, there were several wonderful vacations and many, many memorable professional "highs," but my dominant experience was being "centered but sad." And even while I continued to find my ministry rewarding, part of me began to long for the struggling to be over, even if it meant a premature exit from this world. You might say that death began to have its attractions: I was by no means suicidal, but permanent union with God had a distinct appeal.

It is ironic that one of my constant themes in spiritual direction, writing and teaching is, to use Joseph Campbell's phrase, the importance of "following one's bliss." I am convinced of the importance of each individual following a path of happiness; in fact, one of my gifts as counselor is the ability to help people get in touch with their deepest desires and to find ways of being connected with these desires through work, relationships, prayer, play.... In my own case, however, all the discord in my home was a major impediment to practicing what I preach. I never stopped the activities which I find so life-giving, nor did I neglect any basic spiritual or physical needs—but I did not feel at all blissful, except on an occasional basis.

The steady stretches of contemplative time which are now available to me, the closeness to St. James and to the heart of the city's cultural life, my morning swim at the health club—these have all become part of the "very nice life" I described in an earlier reflection, and have had a positive impact upon my living out of my "bliss." Barely a week ago, however, I received the results from some lab work which indicated "undetermined abnormal cells." The nurse who contacted me assured me that there is no cause for alarm but that further testing will be necessary to rule out any cancer; to my surprise, this was not news I took calmly.

Had I received this information a few months ago—last year, let's say—I would have been completely indifferent to the outcome, and could have lived or died with the same amount of enthusiasm, provided there was no pain involved (my threshold of pain is sadly limited). However, the lab results arrived at a time when things were going relatively well, and when I was beginning to enjoy the art of living. Though, if I am to believe the nurse, there is really no cause for concern, yet my mind went into a spin. How could I even *imagine* a negative outcome when my quality of life had improved so dramatically? How could I even begin to think about dying when, for a change, there is so much to live for?

A few "abnormal cells" hardly amounts to a death sentence, and yet the lab report has given me cause for much reflection. In the first place, it is good to know how my attitude to being alive has shifted from "indifference" to profound gratitude, from mere surviving to delight. Sometimes, it is only when faced with loss that we realize how much we really have, and this has been the case for me. Secondly, I have come to the conclusion that many people have never had even a taste of "bliss," let alone the experience of it. Ideally, it is a quality of life to which everyone should have access, but no one person has a monopoly on it. I no more have a *right* to bliss than my neighbor who died of breast cancer last year at the age of forty-one (she was a few months younger than I), or than my husband's labor foreman who was shot and killed outside their office one Friday afternoon, or than the countless children who never make it into their teens because of violence or poverty. No. Rather than focus on "worst case scenarios" and feel self-pity, I need to remind myself that life is a gift of the moment, to be freely accepted but never clung to or grasped at.

I am at peace with the waiting and with the unknowing. God, who is the Lord of life, the Lord of time, will give me whatever time I need to become that which I am meant to be. If this involves more bliss, I will welcome it gladly; if, however, I am called to eternal bliss, either because of a few unpredictable cells or because of an unexpected turn of events, then I hope I can open my hands as widely as they are presently open to the good things of life. ***Thy will be done.***

# Listening to God

We are so accustomed to imagining that God speaks an almost indecipherable code that we often ignore the divine voice when it is at its clearest. Just as we often dismiss the language of dreams because we have difficulty understanding symbols, so we readily dismiss what it is that God is saying to us, clearly and directly. Sometimes, God's communication with us *is* simple and does not require any process of discernment; in our sophistication, however, we are suspicious when the message seems the most obvious. "It's just the sound of my own voice," we tell ourselves, trying to negate the small voice within. Or, "God would never have said that!"

The more accustomed we are to listening to God, however, the more familiar we are with God's ways of communicating. Sometimes we are overcome by a powerful feeling of some kind; at others, we feel an intuitive hunch gaining validity; at still others, we may hear words in waking or dreaming, bearing their own unmistakable message. Then there are all the significant encounters and meaningful coincidences which form part of daily life, all the surprises and epiphany moments which take us to new places. These, too, are God's way of speaking, of helping us to hear the invitation to fuller living, to deeper understanding....

Three years ago, when difficulties within my family were at their worst, somebody whose judgment I respected urged me to leave. "What are you afraid of?" she asked. "Don't pray *if* you should leave, but *when* you should leave." Even as she spoke, the strong conviction come over me that I was meant to wait. Yes, there had been times when I had thought of leaving, but what resounded throughout my whole being was, "wait." My friend pointed out my resistance, my inability to discern, my refusal to listen to the Holy Spirit, but the more she urged me to leave, the more emphatically I heard, "WAIT."

Part of my obedience to this word involved a complete and absolute rejection of the advice given. Listening to God, it seems, can involve dismissing human advice, even when it is well-intentioned. There was no logical reason for waiting, no grounds to hope that anything would change by waiting, and no indication as to how long this waiting would take. I had no idea as to whether I was dealing with days, months or years—only that waiting was something I *had* to do, regardless of outcome. The word came as a call, as an exercise in obedience, as an invitation to deeper trust and to increased dependency upon God. I did not experience "wait" as a burden so much as challenge, as possibility. "With God all things *are* possible," I reminded myself, remembering other occasions in my life when the impossible had happened. In particular, there was my courtship with Jim some twenty-two years earlier: then my parents had advised me not to see him because I would "not be going to America." After two years of secret meetings and painful deceit, after two years of agonizing over whether or not we should elope, we finally married with their blessing. And that, I told myself, was nothing short of the miraculous....

Even the remembering was God's way of speaking to me. As I recalled the mystery that had brought us together in the first place, as I recalled special moments in our relationship, I was reassured that the waiting was justified. Yes, it was easy to focus on recent hurts and crises and to feel alternately angry and sad, but the past held promise; the past said, "wait." And in the waiting, I felt God's embrace....

"But I need a companion for the journey!" I told God.

"Somebody to help me with the waiting...." I tried thinking of different people I knew who might be appropriate spiritual directors, but none of the names which surfaced seemed a good fit. Then, in prayer, direction came: "Ask Tom." "Tom," I thought to myself, bringing into focus the image of our newly-appointed pastor. "Tom... we're so unalike...and he's not trained in spiritual direction...and he is so burdened with parish work, as it is...." "Ask him anyway," the voice said. "It will be good for both of you. Ask him after Christmas. He will need time to think it over, but he will say yes in the end...."

I have thrived under Tom's companionship. As the waiting has turned into promise and as the promise becomes fulfillment, he has journeyed with me, helping me to continue listening to God's voice and to respond as faithfully as I can to where it may be leading me. And this he can do because he, too, is listening, waiting and responding....

# Back to Basics

Shortly before the "move," a new call surfaced during spiritual direction. I had arrived uncentered, unfocused, and quite flustered about life in general. The frenetic cycle of speaking engagements, traveling and packing had finally caught up with me; we had just moved our son into his own apartment, and I was experiencing many mixed emotions about the seeming breakup of the family. True, Peter had moved out of the house the year before at the age of seventeen, having dropped out of high school, but to see him established in his own place instead of merely rooming with college students and for us to be only days away from the sale of the family home made everything seem more defined; there was no turning back. I found myself grieving over the premature end to family life as we had known it and wondering whether a new house would make a difference in terms of family relationships.

"I don't even know what my 'vocation' is anymore," I complained to Tom. "I feel burned out, unenthusiastic and anxious to get away from all my commitments."

"So where do you think God is calling you?"

"Well, it's always into deeper relationship with God—that's my primary call...."

"Can you be less transcendental?"

"Well, I'm certainly not being called to experience marriage as a vocation, that's for sure," I said heatedly, wondering where the words were coming from.

"So you don't think marriage can be a vocation?"

"Yes, of course I do, I just don't see my marriage as a vocation at this present time. There's still so much healing to be done...."

I was barely out of the rectory when the significance of these words came home to me. Surprised at my own defensiveness, I recognized how I had closed myself from seeing a major part of my life as "call." Because family life had been an area of conflict and unhappiness for many years, I had come to define vocation in terms of ministry—specifically, my work in spirituality. I imagined myself standing at the edge of a circle, reaching out to people through workshops, retreats, lectures, spiritual direction, preaching and writing; I saw the need to return to the center of the circle and to root myself more deeply in home—in my relationship with Jim, with the children, with the domestic side of myself.

I had not deliberately fled the center, or abandoned it. Rather, I had immersed myself in my work because that was where I felt effective and because that was where I found the strength to carry on. Ministry became an ongoing form of renewal, a source of affirmation, a way of connecting with the indwelling God; it energized me and gave me hope in the midst of great pain. It was also a kind of "security blanket"—a guarantee that I *could* survive on my own if I had to, a guarantee that there were enough people who needed my skills that I could always find some kind of employment.

Now, however, it seemed that God was asking me to redirect my energy away from the edge of the circle, toward the center again. Clearly, I was not meant to forsake my ministry, but to re-establish priorities. Instead of being "split" between my professional self and my domestic self, I felt God was inviting me to bring the various aspects of my life into harmony; in this way, I would find energy, security, affirmation and centeredness within *all* that I did.

My initial response was to think that this was the toughest call God had yet sent my way. It meant putting the past behind me and trusting that I could build a different future than the one I had envisioned, right within the heart of my own home. It meant having the flexibility to look for holy companionship within my marriage, and not just in relationships that developed with other ministry professionals. It meant accepting that God's grace would be just as available to me when I was back to "nesting" as it was when I was rushing around doing "God's work."

My attitude began to change. I began to appreciate Peter's immersion in life-learning as he found work, supported himself, took up the electric guitar and began exploring eastern religions. High school had been too confining for him; a year off, and then entry to DePaul via the GED would not be unreasonable, even if this were not the usual way of gaining college entry. Moreover, instead of seeing Peter's move away from home as a fractioning of the family, I now began to appreciate the freedom it had given Jim and me to think about a new beginning. With Alexia just a year away from college, we were almost "empty nesters" and the purchase of a new house that was designed more for couple-life than family-life symbolized this. Moreover, I enjoyed the greater calm that Peter's move had brought with it. Always independent and always old for his age, Peter was ready to be on his own: while we had attempted to hold him back, we paid a terrible price in stress and ongoing conflicts. Curfew had been a major problem, especially as Peter's friends were years older than he was—some in their late twenties. The more we had tried to set limits, the more he had rebelled; Alexia, in turn, had wanted the same liberty, and her defiance led her into several life-threatening situations—one of which landed her in the emergency room with alcohol poisoning (she had drunk a whole bottle of Bailey's at a rock concert) and another in a rehab program for marijuana abuse (she had been caught smoking in the school washroom). This acting out created more cycles of stress, more friction between Jim and me as we struggled with different strategies, generally *reacting* to events and to each other instead of responding with a united front.

But though each of us wishes that things had turned out differently in terms of staying together as a family, the onset of calm has made it possible for us to rediscover what it means to be a couple again; and, as we begin to spend more time together, it has also allowed us to explore the meaning of marriage as vocation and its implications for us as we approach our twenty-second anniversary.

# Go, Feed My Sheep

This morning, I responded to our parish music director's plea for "summer support" by sitting with the choir. Since St. James serves several nearby colleges, we lose our student population during the summer months, and our "regulars" are often away on vacation. Accordingly, numbers are "down" and musical participation decreases noticeably. Colin's new initiative this year has been to invite members of the assembly to become choir members on a "Sunday by Sunday basis." Since I myself will be away for the next three weeks, today was my day to participate.

Except for the fact that a mentally disturbed woman who had forgotten to take her medication sat in the presider's chair for the duration of the homily and then tried to play the piano, the liturgy was uneventful. I found myself able to follow along quite well, and though I missed more reflective time, I enjoyed the experience. I have always loved singing, and so this was a wonderful opportunity to reconnect with an activity for which I no longer have time. In fact, it made me think about *making* time in the future, especially since we now live minutes away from the parish, instead of fifteen miles.

Distracted by events during the homily and by the need to be alert as to musical selections and pages in the hymnals, I did not experience any great revelations or transcendental moments. During the recessional, however, the words struck me with great impact. It was a simple song with the unpromising title of "Go."

The lines I remember at this point—not having access to *Lead Me, Guide Me*—are, "Go ye therefore and teach all nations, Go, go, go.... If you love me, really love me, feed my sheep...." In the space of two or three minutes, my heart and mind were quickly activated.

I have two trips ahead of me: a nine day stay in Saskatoon, Canada, where I will be giving two group retreats as well as a directed retreat, and then, a day after my return, a two week stay in South Africa where I will be visiting my sister, Diana, whom I haven't seen for eight years—not since our youngest sister's wedding in December 1986. When I return to Chicago, my parents will be here from Malta, having just visited New Orleans. It will be an intensive summer and part of me wishes that this were not so.

Part of me—the part that has been enjoying the new house and the proximity of lake, culture and health club—wishes for ordinary days of doing nothing but write and relax; part of me wonders whether the retreat center in Saskatoon or my sister's small town of Mooi River, in Natal, will have such a luxury as a swimming pool. Now that I swim half a mile every morning, I know that I will miss the opportunity for exercise and fear that I will return out of shape—under-exercised and over-fed (as often happens in retreat houses and when one is visiting relatives). I have been feeling so fit and so alive recently that I don't want to have to start health maintenance from scratch.

To return to the hymn. Even as I was singing the words, I felt sent—to be thinking of my own convenience, wishes and schedule when I was going to be in the privileged position of helping others deepen their own encounters with God seemed inappropriate. "Why am I doing this?" I had to ask myself. "Whom am I serving?" Was I simply doing an unimportant piece of free-lance work which would take up more of my summer than I was willing to give, or was I in some way going to be a "missionary"—to Canada, perhaps to South Africa? Was I the one who decided where and when I should go, or did God have any say in the matter? And what about the opportunities for **me** to grow in **my** relationship with God? Perhaps if I spent less time in water and more time in prayer, I would not only feed others but would be fed myself.

That a retreat center in Canada should come across my work and decide to fly me in is so surprising that I have to believe that the Holy Spirit had some say in this. That I was able to schedule in other summer comings and goings so soon after moving is also a mystery to me. Instead of fretting over lost opportunities for swimming and over concerns as to whether the family will survive in my absence, I need to accept the fact that it is to Saskatoon that I am being sent. Whatever awaits me there, God alone knows; for my part, I need to travel lightly, hands open to the new things which will unfold.

# Anxiety Attack or Spiritual Warfare?

The title is ambiguous, as is the content as I move into this reflection. Usually, there is some distance between my personal reflections and my emotional state as I write. I believe it was Wordsworth who once described the poetic process as "emotion recollected in tranquillity"; I am not tranquil—in fact, as I wait for take-off on a Northwest DC-9 headed for Minneapolis where I will change planes, I feel distinctly agitated. I do not want to go.

Very often, when I am about to give a presentation or retreat, events may seemingly conspire against me in the days before—as if to derail me. There have been more occasions than I care to recall when I have left home exhausted, emotionally fragile and seemingly unprepared; then, on arriving at my destination, I find my energy recharges, allowing me to function effectively and to return home feeling renewed. My awareness of this pattern, however, is not helping me this time.

Last week was stressful. Stolen hubcaps, a high speed car chase when I was followed home by three men at midnight, unpleasant medical tests, a travel agent's incompetence, a bout of flu which left me weak and disoriented, and an emotional crisis for my teenage daughter caused by a doctor's crassly insensitive remarks—these are just the "highlights" of the last few days. As the plane begins to roll down the runway, I think of present tense concerns—the fact that Alexia, sixteen, will be traveling by herself to England in my absence and that my parents, in their seventies, will be arriving from Malta and journeying to New Orleans; the fact that between my return from this retreat and my trip to South Africa to visit my sister (whom I haven't seen in eight years), I have only one day back home in Chicago and that my parents will arrive from New Orleans while I am gone again; the fact that Peter, eighteen, who lives alone and has a history of accidents on wheels, rides his bicycle all over the city at all hours; the fact that Jim, my architect husband, is on site every day at gang-ridden projects, with little security now that his labor foreman has been killed.....

Yesterday, my anxiety level peaked into a full-blown panic attack. Already weakened physically, I found myself becoming indecisive, incoherent and weepy. Self-confidence shattered, I wondered how I could face giving the twelve presentations scheduled during the next eight days; I felt totally unprepared. "I don't want to go," I kept telling myself. "Why am I doing this? All I want to do is stay home...." Given my state of mind, my professional involvements and commitment to ministry counted for nothing. Prayer was impossible. Though I tried many of the techniques I would have recommended to directees, nothing worked. I delayed packing until bedtime, but found no release from my angst until, tossing and turning sleeplessly in bed, hours later I prayed this basic prayer: "Lord Jesus, deliver me from the demon of fear...deliver me from the demon of lack of trust... deliver me from the demons of attachment...deliver me from the demon of hopelessness...deliver me...."

Looking down through the clouds at farmland dotted with waterways, I am a little calmer now. I am still afraid and still physically debilitated, but I think I will be able to function— perhaps, with God's help, to inspire. I *would* rather be home, but I have made the commitment to go forward—forward to Saskatoon, forward in terms of my ministry, forward in terms of my marriage. I have no idea where God is calling me. Even as the instinct to "stay put," "to nest," grows stronger, the public invitations become more frequent. "I'm sorry," I told a recent caller. "I can't come in July of next year—I'm only free June 16–25." Seconds later, the phone rang. "Can you come on June 16th, then? We're looking for someone to give a retreat on mysticism...."

The plane begins to lurch. I am in God's hands, as are Jim, Peter, Alexia, my parents.... May the demons keep their distance so that I may be filled with the healing, comforting presence of the Lord of Life, into whose hands I surrender all.

# God Everywhere

Four countries and five plane rides in one week: Saskatoon… Chicago…Rome…South Africa…. Today I am simply sitting, gazing out onto a July winter (yesterday, there was snow up in the Drakensberg mountains), trying to absorb the shifts in seasons and landscapes. It was about six months ago when I began planning this journey—my first—to South Africa. It had been nearly nine years since I had last seen Diana, my eldest sister, and, whether I could afford it or not and in spite of a volatile political situation, I knew I had to see her. And so, while my parents were en route from Malta to Chicago with plans of touring New Orleans, I flew from Chicago to Rome to Johannesburg and then to Durban for a whirlwind visit.

There has been so much to catch up with. I emigrated to the States twenty years ago, and Diana and her family emigrated to South Africa two years later. At first, we managed to plan reunions in Malta, but economic realities interrupted this pattern of meetings. While I managed frequent visits to Malta both with my family and as a leader of student groups from DePaul, the depressed economy kept Diana in South Africa. And so the years rolled by…. Moreover, on those occasions when we had previously met in Malta, there were so many other family members to visit that we had few occasions for *real* conversation—particularly as keeping the children happily occupied was a priority in those days. In effect, then, we have had twenty years of catching up to do.

The days are flying by. I am captivated by this winter landscape—by the tall brown grasses and sugar cane stalks which shine golden in the sunlight; by the vast tracks of blackened land, burned to halt wildfires in the drought months (summer is the rainy season); by the brilliant blossoms of red flame trees and poinsettias, of orange aloe and of countless species I have never seen before. I am intrigued by the cows and donkeys, goats and giant lizards which amble so lazily across the road; by the scores of Zulus who walk mile upon mile to jobs, schools, homes and churches because there is little public transportation; by the rich array of woven baskets, beaded jewelry, carvings and other tribal artifacts....

So far, in the name of photography, I have chased peacocks in public places and giraffes in game reserves, have paid rickshaw drivers to pose with me and have been chased by those who didn't want their photographs taken; I have snapped shots of beautiful babies blanket-wrapped on their mothers' backs, and have regretted "missing the moment" each time a Zulu woman carrying lumber or groceries on her head has walked past. I have photographed shanties and traditional grass huts, have over-indulged in Safari fruits, and I have talked—talked and listened incessantly, usually until 3:00 a.m.

Having missed out on my nephew and niece's growing up, I am anxious to learn something of who they have become. My niece, Nicola, is away at boarding school, but while I have seen little of her, I have pored over her scrapbooks of school awards and community awards, watched family videos and studied the assortment of posters plastered all over her bedroom—presently, *my* room. I like what I see—not just the silver trophies for swimming, hockey, basketball, tennis and judo, not just the certificates for academic excellence, but her zest for life, her spirit, her intensity. It will be good to have her visit Chicago someday, and to show her a larger world than the rural community in which she lives. And my nephew, Patrick—now twenty-one years old and 6' 3". I remember his only visit to Chicago when he was a toddler and how delightful it was to have him spend Christmas with us. I was pregnant with Peter, then, and found myself drawn to the energetic little boy who was curious about everything and relentless in his pursuit of play "parks." My heart still goes out to this young man who towers over me, and I find myself not only taking pride in his talent for photography and stage lighting, but also enjoying his witty humor. Another potential visitor....

Mike, a district supervisor for eighteen or more transport depots since selling their sheep farm, is gone during the week, traveling all over Natal. Most evenings, Diana and I are alone, talking about family life, political changes in South Africa, our hopes and our dreams. This is the greatest gift, this talking. Diana, never a good correspondent, has filled her days and nights with "causes," and it has been quite overwhelming to hear some of the details. For about the last twelve years, for example, she has coordinated civil defense in her small town so that the people are not only prepared to face natural disasters such as floods and fire storms, but also acts of terrorism. Singlehandedly and unpaid, she has organized an ambitious summer program for the primary school children and teenagers of Moor River, so that there has been a daily choice of activities ranging from bikathons to discos, craft workshops to movies, field trips to treasure hunts. Drawing on the skills and talents of locals, tapping into existing events and resources, and persuading local merchants to sponsor different opportunities, Diana has kept children of all races happily involved in experiences which can only help build "the *new* South Africa." At the same time, she also volunteers at St. Theresa's Catholic Church, serving as catechist, liturgist, sacristan and coordinator of the women's group—in addition to working and running a household. Her list of activities makes my own schedule seem light in comparison; I find myself marveling at the generosity of spirit which allows her to give so much....

And so we talk.... There has been little time for silence or for prayer as I usually experience it, but as I listen, I am conscious of the great gift of this visit. In very different contexts, Diana and I do our own share of kingdom building and I find myself giving thanks for the richness of our lives. I have traveled 14,000 miles to learn who my sister is today and to reveal to her who I have become. We are each far from home—if Malta can still be called home. We have each suffered aching homesickness and paid the price of being aliens in the countries in which we reside. We know what it is to raise children without the presence of extended family and to be too far away for anything but the most occasional of phone calls—even in times of crisis. And, in our exile, we have turned to God to be our strength, our support, our reason for being; and God, in God's graciousness, has called us into ministry which brings life and healing, not only to those we serve, but to us, in our woundedness.

# Loaves and Fishes

On my first weekend in Mooi River, we attended the Saturday night European liturgy at the tiny parish of St. Theresa's. The music booklets, donated by a more affluent community, dated from the 1960s, and, as we sang selections without accompaniment, I found myself taken back in time to an era of musical experimentation. The lyrics were curiously sentimental and the heavily male-dominated language seemed archaic. The twenty or so members of the assembly, however, sang with gusto, giving life to music whose strains I barely remembered. Intrigued by the shrill squeaking of bats under the eaves, I found it difficult to be drawn into the homily. Fortunately, Father Tember, the pastor of St. Theresa's and of the Zulu community of St. James, repeated each point several times. There is one that I have carried with me: in preaching on the miracle of the multiplication of loaves and fishes, Father Tember chose to focus on its implications for us today. "Our own resources are often scarce," he reminded us, "but when we surrender them to God, then great miracles can happen." As I reflected on my own resources, I felt the truth of these words. With little or no formal training in most of the things I do, I have to acknowledge that God has indeed worked wonders with what I have to offer. It is a thought which stirs gratitude—and humbleness—in my heart.

The following weekend, we attended the Zulu liturgy at St. James. Though it was scheduled for 9:00 a.m., Father Tember had

warned us not to come before 9:30 a.m. and to expect to be in
church for several hours. Diana explained that many of the people
began walking from farms and settlements as early as 7:00 a.m.
to reach the church and that mass therefore began when most of
them had arrived. As we entered the already full building, others
were also walking in. We sat on a rough wooden bench at the
back, not wanting to draw attention to ourselves as we were the
only Europeans present and I was carrying Nicola's "boom box"
to tape the liturgy. In front of us, rows of women wearing black
hats and purple capes—emblems of a Marian solidarity—were
jammed shoulder to shoulder; across the aisle sat the men and
children; here and there, women, with babies tied to their backs
by colorful blankets, sat among their purple-clad sisters. There
was coughing, crying, whispers and fidgeting and then,
unexpectedly, a lone voice intoned a refrain. The response then
and after every other cue was electric. As in the European church,
there were no accompanying instruments, but here in this poorest
of gatherings, voices played with harmony, resounded with deep
rhythms, spontaneously created soulful choral arrangements. I
taped what I could, joined in the "Alleluias" and handclapping,
and though I understood none of the words, I was profoundly
moved by the experience of heart-song.

The prayers of intercession were powerful. The women wept
out their petitions so fervently and so powerfully that there was
no doubt as to their sincerity. I found myself thinking how
antiseptic and sterile most "white" liturgies were in comparison
and how much we from the first world have to learn about "soul"
from those whose living conditions place them firmly in the third.
Of course, South Africa can hardly be ranked as a third world
country any more than the U.S., but whether one lives in a shanty
town or in the projects, whether one lacks electricity and running
water or is dehumanized by gang warfare in hallways reeking of
urine, one is still experiencing third world conditions.

When mass was over, there was a procession in honor of the
feast of the Sacred Heart. Everybody paid R. O.50 for a treasured

candle and, one by one, we passed the flame of faith down the line, repeatedly relighting our candles as the wind just as frequently puffed them out. There was smiling and laughter and, when the wax began to drip onto my hand, somebody offered me a scrap of brown paper to use as a candle holder.

Loaves and fishes had multiplied at St. James. Here, all gave out of their poverty, enriching the entire community. Here, the barefoot and the barely shod gathered in praises so loud that it is a wonder the church's tin roof stayed on. Diana and I had reservations at a German restaurant and so had to leave after the procession. Part of me wishes we could have stayed to share in a simple community meal at St. James.

# No Delight

Something about me has changed. With all the transitions and traveling of the last few months, I feel as though my soul is finally beginning to catch up with my body. House guests have left, my suitcases are stored away, the last wall hangings and photographs are in place and I am back at work—back at DePaul, back seeing private directees, and back running *Fanning the Flame of Faith*, the archdiocesan formation program for lay spiritual companions. Everything is as it should be and yet something has changed: I no longer have any enthusiasm for anything.

At first, I told myself that I was recovering from almost 30,000 miles of traveling, following a house move and an intensive academic schedule. When several weeks passed and my enthusiasm did not return, I thought that I was still grieving over family goodbyes and reawakened homesickness; this, too, however, became an unlikely excuse. I noticed that everything I had felt passionate about no longer held much meaning. In contrast to the heightened emotions I experienced during the summer, I now feel nothing. In fact, the very work which has been so life-giving over the years and which has sustained me in so many ways has now become a burden. I do not want to meet with directees, give workshops or retreats, teach or preach; I look forward to nothing—neither to visiting friends nor to upcoming trips; I simply want to stay home, keep my house in order, swim and write—but not too rigorously.

I named my condition "spiritual malaise"; because I have been blessed so abundantly in the last few months, I began to feel ungrateful and guilty, especially since prayer has held no attraction. What little energy I had has gone into sewing a tunic by hand (because I never learned how to use a sewing machine) and into baking banana bread and apple date bread and zucchini bread and poppy seed cake and lethal chocolate chip bars.... I have become "domestic" with a vengeance....

It was only this morning that I finally came to understand some of the dynamics at work. The clue, actually, has lain on my desk for several weeks. Over the summer, George, a retreat leader and graphoanalyst, sent me a lengthy report on a handwriting sample I had given him. Intrigued by the way I link many of my illegible words, George had tried valiantly to make sense of my character on the basis of my writing. While there was much I appreciated about his observations, one point seemed to hit home more than any of the others: that I am a "highly emotionally responsive person." Now, this in itself is no revelation; I have known for years that my capacity to feel things at an extraordinarily deep level has been both an asset and a liability. The importance of George's comments is that they remind me of how extensively I am ruled by my feelings. In the past, I have done what I have done because I loved doing it—not out of obligation or necessity but out of pure delight. Delight, in fact, has pushed me into areas of creative and intellectual exploration and has helped me to juggle impossible schedules when mere "good will" would have failed. Delight has given me energy and enthusiasm, passion and conviction, eloquence and charisma. And now, it seems, delight is gone.

About two weeks ago, I visited Tim who supervises the different areas of my life I name "ministry." Always challenging, he had pointed out a certain willfulness on my part. I think I have successfully blocked out the specifics of what he said, but he indicated that I needed to pay attention to the relationship between my work and self-gratification. Now, as I read over

George's comments, I feel I have gained some clarity: I have to admit that up until the present moment, much of my commitment to ministry, much of my sense of calling has had to do with enjoyment and self-fulfillment. Ministry comes naturally to me, almost effortlessly; it feels like an extension of myself and makes me more alive than anything else that I do.

If Tim were here as I write, we would have a conversation which I think would go something like this:

**Me:** "So you're saying that I need to look at my sense of commitment?"

**Tim:** "I'm not saying you are not committed, but that you need to examine your motives more closely. You derive a great deal of pleasure from your work—"

**Me:** "But is that wrong?"

**Tim:** "Not at all, but your primary reason for ministry needs to be that God has called you to it, not that you enjoy it."

**Me:** "Well, I certainly do have a sense of call—I would never have become a spiritual director if I didn't, nor would I have gone into campus ministry...."

**Tim:** "But even when we first began talking about your gifts, you spoke of your intense feelings of frustration when you were not able to use them. Frustration often comes from the ego...."

**Me:** "So you're saying that I derive more pleasure from doing godly things than from God?

**Tim:** "I wouldn't have put it so strongly, but I suppose I am saying something like that. Perhaps if we centered on participating in Christ's delight in and through our ministry and the ministry of the whole church, there would be fewer moments of letdown."

**Me:** "I think I understand what you are saying—I'm beginning to wonder whether I only do those things that I enjoy doing...."

**Tim:** "There you have it—you pour yourself wholeheartedly into everything you do, but would you continue to do this if there were nothing in it for you? It's just a question...."

Even writing this imaginary conversation is helpful. Tim's "question" challenges me to see whether it is indeed commitment or self-gratification which prompts me to invest myself in ministry. If I am honest with myself, I have to admit that both are realities for me, and that I am most effective when both come into play. However, I know myself well enough to be able to say that even when delight is absent, I will still respond to the situation at hand, getting done whatever has to be done, albeit with some reluctance. Take my present situation. Whereas in the past I would look forward to each day because I was meeting with a particular person or teaching a particular class, now I study my calendar with complete indifference, not wanting to **do** anything. This coming Sunday, for example, I am scheduled to preach at the Mass of the Holy Spirit at the university, but my gut feeling is, "The gospel says it all—there's no need for me to add anything." No doubt the liturgy will go smoothly and people will be moved by what I have to say, but, most likely, I myself will derive little pleasure from my contribution. Significantly, however, I believe that commitment will carry me in the absence of delight.

Now that I understand the close connections between delight and commitment in my ministerial undertakings, I am more at peace. It is clear that the way to motivate myself is to remember that what is primary is that "God's work" should be done, not that I should "get anything out of it." I need to also remember that in each situation in which I minister, I am enabling others to encounter Christ through my presence. And this, I am sure, is what Tim would say should be my only concern....

# Resting in God's Embrace

Distance and intimacy, invitation and seeming abandonment—these are all characteristics of the divine dance of love as I have experienced it. At some moments, God's presence lures, entices and woos, beckoning us into responding wholeheartedly; at others, there is neither movement nor music, neither ecstasy nor consolation—only our fidelity. As I continue to explore the meaning of "no delight," I am aware of how my own responses to this time of desert seem to be bringing about a new way of being—perhaps a process of conversion.

In the times when I have felt most alive, I have awakened with a sense of hopefulness, a sense of expectancy. I have gone forward into my day with enthusiasm, enjoying each activity and feeling God's presence illuminating me, wherever I am. On such days, I am fully aware of the ways God uses me to reach others; without delight, however, I feel like a shell of myself. I resent interruptions—particularly of the telephone variety—and basically want to be left alone. Instead of experiencing ministry as privilege, it seems like a burden. Even writing is no longer coming easily. Ironically, this is a time when I not only have fan mail to respond to, but former directees and former students are constantly seeking me out, either for specific advice or for a chat to catch up with where life has taken them. For my part, I feel as though I have nothing to give. Touched by others' affection for me, humbled by their respect for what I have to say and their trust in my input, I feel burdened by the demands, wearied by constantly being "on." Even though I make the effort to be present to their needs in the time available, I often have a sense that I am giving less than they hoped to receive, that I have somehow short-changed them. My fear is that they came to me hungry and left as hungrily as they came because I was incapable of being fully present in the moment. Phone calls come in my writing time and in my praying time, in the times I am trying to be present to my family, in moments of trying to catch up with household chores, or in that vulnerable moment of first walking through the front door after a full day at DePaul. People often say, "Is this a good time for you?" or "When would be a good time to reach you?" but the truth is that there is seldom a good time—there are always so many pressing needs, so many things to accomplish, whether this involves running out to the grocery store or planning a class for the next day. I **do** screen phone calls via my answering machine, but this only means that I have calls to return at some later time. Again, I want to be left alone; I hunger for empty spaces in which I am responsible only for myself....

Faced with the possibility that my "condition" could deteri-orate to the point that I would be incapable of getting my work done, I have tried to reshape my attitude. Each time I am going to meet with someone for spiritual direction or counseling, I not only ask God to work through me, in spite of my unwillingness, but I also remind myself that I am standing (or sitting) in the place of Christ and that I therefore need to welcome each person as he would. Though the idea of meeting with someone for about an hour presently holds no appeal, I keep in mind that I am doing holy work which needs to be done. I am not accepting any more directees off campus and I am limiting my free-lance work to Thursdays; this is part of my attempt to give myself the space I need for my own inner work. At the same time, however, I feel a sense of responsibility toward those people I am already walking with as spiritual companion. Were I really "burned out," then terminating my work with them might be appropriate, but I am not dealing with burn-out. My prayer during each session becomes, "For your sake only, Lord...."

Teaching is much the same. There is a certain energy I usually receive as I facilitate conversation around significant themes, sharing some of my own experience and knowledge with my students. For me, much of what happens in the classroom is spontaneous—context appropriate, yes, but nevertheless unplanned. It seems that different skills surface as needed, creating an atmosphere that is stimulating, innovative and challenging. Now, because I can no longer count on this happening, I need to make a note before class not only of topics to cover but of different strategies to employ while teaching. I doubt whether any former students would notice a substantial change in my method, but I am conscious of no longer being carried by my enthusiasm.

And prayer, too, has shifted. It is discipline and discipline alone that draws me to pray these days. Whereas in the past there have been times when I could hardly wait to move into silence and to simply be with God, now nothing draws me except the sense that prayer is all I have to hold onto. Most of the time, I feel nothing and say nothing. Occasionally, at eucharist, I feel moved by the ritual words and gestures, but in my private prayer there is seldom the sense of union to which I had grown so very accustomed and for which I long so passionately. Prayer has become a descent into emptiness, into darkness, into a nothingness that is also pregnant. I do not feel, but I know—know beyond all doubting—that Something other than myself is present. I believe—without there being any dramatic proof that this is not merely wishful thinking on my part—that the Something desires my fidelity to both prayer and ministry, and that I am responding to the challenge appropriately.

At times, strong feelings of sadness wash over me. I find myself mourning over the usual things—the changes in family life which began with Peter's departure cause especially strong reactions. Two weeks ago, he entered DePaul as a freshman, having been out of school for eighteen months; his enthusiasm for learning is a delight, but when he stops by my office to let me know how things are going, or when he calls me at night to fill me in on the day's events and to share with me some new insights on a philosophical question, I wistfully wonder what it would be like were he living at home. Or when Alexia sits at the piano after more than two years of ignoring it and I hear her passion and talent try to express themselves with fingers that are no longer flexible, I want to weep. In happier days, her music-making used to fill our home—our old home. As her fingers flew over the keys, making the very walls reverberate, I felt my spirit soar and, in the privacy of my study, my feet began to move until I was as fluid as the music and my body had become my prayer. Then the music stopped, abruptly and without explanation.

Memories surface of the last few years of struggling—years without music or dancing—but if I successfully banish those, I find myself thinking of my scattered family of origin and of the thousands of miles which separate us. These emotions quite outshadow any sense of satisfaction I feel for my ministry—in fact, were it not that I value the people I serve, I would feel that what I do is largely irrelevant. About five years ago, I wrote a lengthy poem for my doctoral project; this presented biblical narratives from a woman's perspective and in one—my story of a female Jonah—I lament being snatched from my dreams of "wellside gossip and women's ways." Prophetically enough, this is how I feel today—how rich it would have been to have had ordinary days of seeing my nephews and nieces grow up, or to have had more leisure to spend with my own children instead of ministering to the world at large, or of having more time to spend in service to the needy.... Where has time gone? I ask myself; how did my children grow so quickly while I was battling with vocational issues and survival issues?

When tears fall, I feel God's embrace. I hear nothing, see nothing, receive no dramatic insights, but I know God's heart is present to my heart. There is no reassurance that this state of "no delight" is temporary, but my hunch is that "no delight" is yet another dimension of the purgative process. I am neither fighting "no delight" nor asking God to let it pass. I am entering into it without raging or objecting and almost feel indifferent to its duration, painful though it is. I would hardly describe myself as being happy or "fulfilled," and yet I experience a certain amount of peace, the feeling of being held. Were I to define who God is for me at this time in my life, I would have to say that God is "No Delight" or "Absence of Joy." **This** is the God who embraces me.

# Absolute Sweetness

Having named God as "No Delight" and "Absence of Joy" in my last reflection, I felt drawn to prayer. As the need for stillness came over me, I abandoned my manuscript and sat down on the futon, unclear as to where this need came from. It was ironic, I told myself, that I should respond so quickly when I had spent the last half hour or so lamenting the vicissitudes of life. But I sat, and waited....

Almost immediately, a sensation of warmth came over me—an exterior warmth which also warmed me internally, so that I had an incredible sense of well-being. I felt a much higher than usual state of consciousness, a state of becoming filled with light and surrounded by light. My spirit soared; my body throbbed with responsiveness.

"Don't think you have succeeded in defining me," said the voice deep within myself. "You have named me as "No Delight" and "Absence of Joy" but these names represent only a fragment of the truth of who I am. I am also "Absolute Sweetness.""

I wanted to object to this new name that was so far from my recent experience. Yes, I was tasting "absolute sweetness" now and had often done so before, but I knew the experience would fade, leaving me craving for more sweetness still. Within the hour, in fact, I had returned to ordinary consciousness. By the next day, the feeling of extraordinary peacefulness had completely disappeared. Once again, I encountered "No Delight."

103

Part of me wondered what purpose the revelation of the day before had served, beyond reminding me that my definitions of God were always too limited and too rooted in my own feelings. I had tasted an alternative reality and this had deepened my hungers more than it had given me hope that things could ever change. Moreover, whereas I have often been caught up in what I can only describe as a moment of ecstasy, with God as its source and subject, my encounter with "Absolute Sweetness" had not taken me to the deepest kind of unitive experience, but had left me waiting for what did not come. My expectations had grown as the warmth became more intense, but I was left only with the memory of John of the Cross' warnings about the dangers of developing a "spiritual sweet tooth," a craving for gratification rather than for God.

Yes, I **do** believe that God is "Absolute Sweetness," and I believe because there have been times in my life when I have experienced this sweetness for hours—and sometimes days—on end. In the past, I have purged myself of the expectation that sweetness **should** come my way, that I had any right to it, or that I could control its happening through my own desire or asking. I learned to accept that "sweetness" comes from God purely as gift, without any merit on the part of the recipient; its shadow side, I discovered, is that it can make people desire the overwhelming experience more than relationship with God: in other words, the "danger" is that we can mistake experience for ultimate reality.

It would be dishonest of me to claim that I am indifferent to the ways God chooses to approach me. Given a choice, I would much rather know God as "Absolute Sweetness" than as "No Delight"; given a choice, I would much rather live in constant heightened consciousness than in a state of ordinary contentment. At the moment, I experience neither.....

But an experience in supervision again comes to mind as so often is the case when I need to be challenged. My sessions with Tim began as occasions for exploring my feelings and reactions in relationship to the work I was doing in spiritual companioning; as time went on, however, I looked to Tim to "supervise" the vocational issues I presented—issues not simply related to the ministry of spiritual direction but also to the other areas of ministry with which I am involved. I use our time together not only for purposes of consultation and self-reflection, but also to examine my sense of call, as, for example, the call to more public ministry. During one of our meetings, I lamented how I felt "swallowed" by DePaul and also by my wider commitments. I expressed the desire to retire in "four years" (at age forty-seven) so that, having more time for prayer and for writing, I would be more available for "Absolute Delight" when it should come my way.

"And how do you know that this is what God wants for you?" asked Tim.

"It's a question of following my bliss—that's surely what God intends?" I responded defensively. "I am tired of feeling burnt-out and over-extended. I'm tired of being 'on' for whoever happens to knock at my door or to phone me. Sometimes I feel as though I want to go into hiding, just to protect my private space. I have a high need for both silence and solitude...."

"But does this mean that **God** wants you to retire?" persisted Tim. "**You** are the one who wants more time for quiet and for prayer. **You** are the one who wants more time alone, but have you ever thought that God may be reaching you in your busyness or that God may have other goals for you? I am still hearing willfulness here—yes, one needs to be prudent about scheduling events and about taking care of physical needs, but perhaps God is calling you to be 'poured out' at this time, to be spent for the sake of the kingdom. When we put ourselves in God's hands, then Providence provides the things we need—the renewal, the experience of God's intimacy, the knowledge we need to share, and, at times, even 'delight.'"

"So even wanting more extended time for prayer can be willful?"

"Anything can be—we always come back to the same old

questions, 'What does God desire for us at this moment? What is the work that only **we** can do at this time?' We have to remind ourselves that ministry is not a career option but a calling, and sometimes the conditions aren't the ones we would have chosen for ourselves."

"This feels pretty radical," I said. "I assumed that wanting more prayer time was reasonable, that wanting to be less frenetically busy was spiritually healthy, that making plans for a more contemplative lifestyle indicated my deep yearning for God...."

"And all of this **is** good, provided we don't fool ourselves as to who is doing the wanting. God can be close to us wherever and whenever God chooses—not necessarily in a retreat center or some other out of the way place. God can find us in whatever moment we find ourselves, but we must keep honest: exactly where does **God** hope to find us? It's not a matter of where **we** want to be found...."

It is quite possible, I remind myself, that God does not want to be experienced as "Absolute Sweetness" at this time. It's quite possible that God wishes to present me with another experience of Godself. It's quite possible that God wants me to experience desolation even though I interpret this as a negative. It is quite possible that God wants me to bend my will to God's will....

# God-Bearer

"Perhaps God is inviting you to something new," said Tom as I shared with him my experience of "no delight" in a spiritual direction session. "Perhaps this is an invitation to deeper relationship...." In my state of aridity, Tom's suggestions during spiritual direction were all I could cling to. I found myself wondering why God couldn't find more palatable ways of extending invitations. Yes, I understood the value of the path of purgation and felt its familiar dust beneath my feet, but I did not like it.

There was anger in my prayer. "Well, God, where's the invitation? What am I supposed to be learning from this darkness?" Almost immediately, an image surfaced: that of a woman praying before a tabernacle. I identified the woman, who was deep in meditation, as myself and the prayer space as my parish, St. James. Staying with the image, I found myself probing its meaning. The woman, I decided, was the "keeper of the tabernacle." Her task was to dwell in the holy of holies, keeping vigil, protecting the sacrament, offering worship....

"So is this what I'm being called to?" I asked. "How much time am I supposed to spend before the tabernacle? Is this a call to constant devotion and, if so, how am I supposed to have the time to do this?" Given my schedule, commitments and inclinations, the ministry of permanent adoration held little appeal and did not seem very practical. I thought of Holy Thursday, 1995, the most recent time I had spent before the Blessed Sacrament, keeping vigil after the evening liturgy. Then, I had wanted to focus exclusively on Jesus' suffering and to companion him in the garden. To my disappointment, I had great difficulty in abandoning my own issues and had to work very hard at visualizing leaving *my* agenda wrapped up in a bundle at the threshold to Gethsemane.

Perhaps this is an invitation for the future, I thought to myself; perhaps it's meant to remind me of my dream to have a retreat house one day—a place of quiet where people can come for healing.... From the vantage point of "no delight," I did not find this possibility engaging.

Even as my thoughts were spinning, yet another image came into view: the woman and tabernacle merged into one and the same reality; only the woman's form remained. Now the invitation seemed to be nothing less than to **be** the tabernacle; in other words, it seemed as though God was reminding me that my own being could become the holy of holies, that God did not desire to reside in some gilded container, but desired, instead, to find shelter within the human heart—and, in this instance, within me. While I had felt somewhat irritated by the earlier invitation, this one was deeply moving. For me to become tabernacle meant that God was inviting me into deeper intimacy, into greater attentiveness to the divine presence, into constant prayer. Instead of being drawn to an external symbol, I was to heighten my consciousness of the Christ within. I thought of the constant repetition of the "Jesus Prayer" and wondered whether that would be an appropriate way of remembering my role as "receptacle." I realized that this new "call" involved being available to God at all times. "But how?" I asked myself. "How can one be prayerfully present to God while meeting the incessant obligations of family and work? Is God pushing me to quit my job at this time when, financially, I need to stay put? Is this invitation something to which I can actually respond?" For several days, I found myself playing with the implications of this image. While sitting or kneeling before a tabernacle belonged to the realm of impossibility, the new image allowed for mobility and continued involvement in the external world; on the other hand, there was no easy solution to the question of how to maintain consciousness in action.

A third image evolved. The word "Theotokos" came to me, the Orthodox name for Mary, Bearer of God. In my imagination, I saw an icon of Mary—dark, severe, with sad piercing eyes which seemed to look beyond me. But while the iconographic Mary traditionally holds the age-old child in one arm, pointing to him with the other, this Mary was with Child; her parted cloak revealed a cross section of her womb in which the regal Child was enthroned, fully clothed, facing me, right hand raised in a gesture of blessing. It was immediately clear to me that a new invitation **had** been extended, that I was being invited to participate in the work of God-bearing begun by Mary, but extended by Christians everywhere. As one who has never had a strong sense of connection to Mary, I found this symbol ironic but strangely moving.

Becoming Theotokos meant more than simply being a sacred vessel. The second image of woman as tabernacle reflected relationship between the human and the divine, but it was not as intimate an image as that of Mother and Child. In the image of Theotokos, one of the implications was not only that the Mother provided the Child with a safe space—a sanctuary—but that the lives of both were intricately connected: the divinity of the Child and the humanity of the Mother were one and the same reality; through the Mother's physical presence, the God within shone forth in glory, but the Mother was illuminated, even as she pointed beyond herself.

The image has taken on one more level of meaning for me. Having returned to the image during prayer, I found that the Christ Child dissolved into the brilliant blue of our planet, as seen from outer space. It was Earth as described by astronauts on their journey moonward or as captured in a satellite-transmitted photograph—Earth in all her beauty and in all her radiance. The Cosmic Christ, I reminded myself, indeed contains all things and is Lord over all; the Cosmic Christ is indeed involved in the re-creation of the universe, and our task, as co-creators, is to be involved in this process. I was filled with wonder and awe.

To be Theotokos, a bearer of Christ and revealer of Christ at the deepest level possible—this was the call as I experienced it. As I allowed the image and its implications to take root in my heart, I was filled with new energy, new hopefulness, a new easiness in praying. "No Delight" became "All Delight." Clarity and purpose surged through me; contemplation once again became a natural "activity." And I began to hear other calls—the invitation to help others become Theotokos, the invitation to renew the church by extending my work of spiritual formation to as many people as possible, both clergy and laity.... **Theotokos**...

# Eucharist as Sacred Remembering

As I reflect on the significance of being a Christ-bearer, many themes of the inner life coalesce for me. Though I see Christ-bearing as extending beyond eucharistic piety, I find myself returning to my understanding of eucharist, and this, in turn, is related to why I stay in the church, to the theme of servanthood, and to the importance of being Christocentric.

Yesterday, as has happened so often before, I found myself explaining to my students why it is that I haven't changed denominations. They had spent much of the class period citing reasons for their own alienation from the Catholic Church (incidentally, the three reasons most frequently given are "hypocrisy," "sex scandals" and "sexism"); then, as might be expected, their attention focused on why I, a seemingly liberated woman, have managed to stay in the church. "It all comes down to eucharist," I explained. "It is an important part of my own spirituality, as are the riches of the liturgical seasons. I would miss the sounds and symbols too much...."

I went on to discuss my theology of eucharist. Drawing on the work of Mircea Eliade (as, for example, *The Sacred and the Profane* and *Myth and Reality*), I explained how the purpose of all ritual is to help us remember and that to forget is "sacrilege." Eliade's scholarship reflects the reality that the power of rites enabled archaic peoples to repeat what had happened in "the beginning," to imitate the life-giving actions of their ancestors, to participate in the renewal of the cosmos. They did not simply commemorate glorious and wonderful deeds, but made these deeds their own. Through ritual, they were able to overcome the limitations of chronological time and to participate in primordial time, the time of the beginning.

By extension, then, we could say that the celebration of eucharist allows us to experience sacred time; without displacing linear time—history, the moment in which we find ourselves— we also participate in the story of Jesus. What we "do" Sunday after Sunday and every time we celebrate the eucharist is not something we primarily "do" for God, but action which sustains us and empowers us. Through the liturgical repetition of the words and actions of Jesus and through the liturgical cycle of his life, sacred time and linear time become one. We are no longer defined or determined by chronological time—that is, by the events of our personal histories or of our society or even of our world—but we become intimately involved in Jesus' life.

Though occupied Palestine was racked and riddled with its own share of misery and has continued to be so even today, yet there, in Jesus, the reign of God was made manifest; there was a breakthrough of the divine into human history; the world was created anew. Choosing Isaiah 61 as his text, Jesus announced his ministry as a time of good news—a time of healing, freedom and rebuilding. Through his presence, people found wholeness of mind, body and spirit. They learned what it was to live with Emmanuel—with God among them—and they learned the transforming power of love, its impact upon the most desperate of circumstances, the most hardened of hearts. The brief moment in history recorded in the gospels, then, was truly a "sacred time" which we remember at eucharist, with gratitude.

Religious ceremonies, as Eliade pointed out, are "festivals of memory"; sin is forgetting divine generosity. We need liturgy to remind us who we are and where we have come from, to imprint upon our hearts the memory of God's saving power. One way in which we recall sacred time is through the stories we tell and retell whenever we gather in Jesus' name. These stories describe God's intervention in time and predict the glory that is to come. As people living after the event of incarnation, we break bread and share wine until that day when all things will be made whole. Eucharist, then, is our way of remembering. Each time we celebrate the eucharist, we proclaim that Christ has died, Christ is risen and Christ will come again. Eucharist forms us and gives us our identity—that is, to become Christ for the world. As Paul writes in 1 Corinthians 12:13, "In one spirit we were all baptized, Jews as well as Greeks, slaves as well as citizens, and one spirit was given us all to drink." Each time we celebrate the eucharist, we not only remember Jesus, reminding ourselves through word and action of the mysteries of salvation, but we pledge to become Christ for the world and, in so doing, accept the selves we have become and are in the process of becoming.

If we understand eucharist to mean participating in the life of Jesus, then we must also participate in his servanthood. Jesus told his disciples that those who want to be the greatest of all have to be the servants of all: to follow him means to "be for others," to engage in feet-washing. Though, like Peter, our first response may be one of shock, if we stretch our imaginations we can see there are many ways of washing feet, few of them literal. Feet washing happens whenever we extend ourselves for others in Jesus' name, whenever we humble ourselves, whenever we allow ourselves to experience inconvenience for the sake of another.

Servanthood means that we allow ourselves to be available to Christ so that his work may be done. It involves a complete and utter stripping of the ego so that we will be open to wherever God may be calling us. What we do we must do for Christ's sake, not to draw attention to ourselves, or to display our talents, or to receive a reward of some kind. Rather, our only concern should be to love, love, love—and love some more. Being a servant—a washer of feet—is both a privilege and a responsibility. Ultimately, it means allowing ourselves to be broken for the world, to be life for the world. Just as Jesus poured out his life for the life of many, so we, too, need to be willing to pour ourselves out....

Ritual meals have always been a source of not only remembering sacred events and participating in them, but also of gaining strength. By remembering sacred story and sacred action and participating in both through receiving the bread and the wine, we also remember who we are—not just particular people bearing particular names and living in particular places, but, rather, people made in the image of Christ. Our deepest selves are not determined by our histories or by our salaries or by the positions we hold—or do not hold—but by the extent to which we mirror Christ. By participating in eucharist, we increase Christ's life within us and we discover that there is more to us than our hopes, desires, petty grudges or ambitions, or even our suffering.

This is something we need to remember not just in terms of our own prayer, but also in terms of the many others with whom we worship. Eucharist is soul food that enables us to make horizontal connections with each other. Praying in community reminds us that the eucharist is the celebration of the whole church. Through the presence of differing others, we are reminded of those absent people whom we tend to forget—the world's poor, hungry and imprisoned; society's outcasts; the ill and the dying; the victims of war and violence; the lonely and the bereaved.... What we "do" as a community, then, we do in the name of the world, and not just in our name. This "connecting" humanizes us, deepens our compassion, helps us to live the paschal mystery....

As my students began to get the picture that there is more to eucharist than the individual moment of receiving, I explained that many of the ways we were taught as children were inadequate accounts of what happens at the Lord's table. Although there *is* an immediate encounter between the living Lord and ourselves, eucharist involves more than our being present to divine presence. It involves our gratitude for all that we have and are, the offering of ourselves for the world, our pledge to become Christ for others. Receiving the eucharist is not something of a few minutes' duration. It is not limited to the length of time it takes to swallow bread and wine and to say "Amen" to each; rather, the "Amen" extends eucharist into every moment of our lives. It is our promise to be Christ for others in whatever ways we ourselves relate to him—as healer, teacher, companion, listener, prophet, social activist.... Whatever ways Christ is most real for us are the ways we can best be him for others; whoever Christ is for the world, we need to be also—in whatever ways our circumstances allow. We must be concerned with the eucharistic pattern of our lives, not just with the moment of receiving.

The food we receive nourishes us; at the same time, it sends us forth to be food for others. The responsibility and privilege extend to all. What we receive, we must be; the actions we repeat, we must make our own. The memorial meal, the sacrifice on Calvary and the emptying of the tomb never cease precisely because we refuse to forget. By remembering, by helping others to remember, by repeating sacred action, we are continuing God's work of divinizing the planet. God became one of us so that we might become divine. Wherever we are, whatever our situation, we can be the presence of Christ. Thanks be to God.

# God's Absurdity

In my study, not far from my various certificates and diplomas, are two 8 x 10 photographs of myself as a small child—perhaps two years old at the most. The child's mouth is puckered into a grin that can hardly contain her delight in life; plump and cherubic, she is ready to embrace not only her sister's dolls' house (the sister being safely at school), but anything else that comes her way. Her vitality, her intensity, her mischievous gaze all convey the sense that she is strong-willed—strong enough of character to set her own course, to follow her own path, to be her unique self. Of course, I am prejudiced in my interpretation of these two simple black and white photos. As I gaze upon them, I see qualities in the child which now manifest themselves in my adult self. It is with a sense of awe, of wonder, of gratitude that I recognize how far God has brought me since the capturing of those images.

If, as a toddler, I embodied qualities I now appreciate as an adult, and if I seemed to be blessed with creativity and strength of character, my growing-up experiences did nothing to enhance my natural gifts; on the contrary, I was isolated, lonely, culturally estranged, intellectually deprived and over-fed. Let me explain. As I have mentioned elsewhere, I grew up in two cultures, moving every two years between England and Malta until middle school, when we settled in Malta; neither place was home. Having Anglo-Maltese parentage, I was too tall and too fair

skinned to be Maltese, and too much of a brunette to be
English—not only did my dark hair give me away, but my
Mediterranean eyes betrayed me as a "foreigner." My English
was impeccably correct—perhaps *too* correct for me to be
considered a "local" in Hampshire and Surrey, the two English
counties where we lived, and, of course, being Catholic was
another strike against me—real patriots were Anglicans. In
Malta, on the other hand, I never made the effort to learn Maltese
and so found myself excluded from many conversations. My
maternal grandmother, for example, spoke very little English and
I never really got to know her because of the language barrier. I
remember hours and hours of family gatherings in which all the
adults spoke Maltese, while my sisters and I ate away the time,
out of boredom (there were always wonderful cakes, cookies and
homemade ice cream wherever we went); I began to equate
visiting relatives with "binge time" and ended up overweight but
not obese.

When I was nine or ten, I did not know what it was to have
playmates, and the children with whom I went to school seldom
let me participate in their games because I was perceived as
"different." I found myself wearing a mask of cheerful
indifference, though, in reality, I was mortified to be seen on my
own at recreation, and often ended up hiding in the restrooms.

When I finally *did* discover the joys of friendship at a Catholic
day school in England, it was time to move back to Malta again. I
had just come to delight in some of my creative skills and
leadership abilities, and, for the first time in my experience, had
freedom of movement. My father was busy commuting to the
London War Office, while my mother was occupied with my
younger sisters, Patricia and Anne, who were five and newborn,
respectively; Diana, fifteen, was preparing for her school leaving
certificate exams, and so there was little supervision. With a band
of ten year olds in tow, I hiked along canals, biked down country
roads, explored ancient cemeteries, visited horses in clover fields,
put on puppet shows for the neighborhood, dug up hog bones for

my archeological society, picnicked on cattle farms (and got chased both by fierce bulls and angry boars), and practiced jumping over open sewers—until my friend, Helen, slipped and fell, and brought such a nauseating stench back to my home that there was no mistaking our adventure.

The news that we were returning to Malta was hard. I vowed that as soon as I possibly could, I would return to England on my own and, having wept copiously all the way back to Malta—we spent two weeks touring Europe—sullenly made up my mind to disassociate myself from anything and everything Maltese. I saw our return as an end to my freedom and to my range of activities. Even at ten, I felt there was no future for me on the island, particularly as Maltese women—I should say, Maltese *ladies* that I had encountered—neither worked, volunteered, had meaningful friendships, nor pursued any kind of intellectual life. Of course, there must have been exceptions, but from my point of view being female in Malta was tantamount to having no rights at all.

At the same time, all the school changes and cultural differences had a negative impact on my education; it seemed that I was always trying to catch up with one subject or another, especially languages and math. I was an avid reader—mostly of my father's childhood World War I stories, and of anything British. Fascinated by our Scottish family name, I delved into highland history, practiced my Scottish accent until it was quite authentic, and flaunted tartans and heraldic jewelry. None of this, however, made up for my strong impression that I was somehow mentally deficient and not "college material." A kind of existential despair set in, intensified by the fact that my new classmates were into bras and boys, while I viewed my own sexual development—which, at that time, amounted to a few dark hairs under my armpits—with abhorrence.

It was not until I was about fourteen that I again got in touch with my own creativity. As a boarder at the Sacred Heart Convent, I became involved in drama, archeology, folk singing and many other activities. Encouraged by a history teacher from Yorkshire, I developed a fascination for medieval and renaissance history, and read extensively to supplement class work. I began to realize that I might have some academic potential after all, but could not see any way of returning to England to study—preferably to Oxford—which was still my goal.

At about the same time, my spiritual life became very intense. I found myself drawn to prayer on a regular basis—to morning mass, even on optional days, to afternoon benediction, to compline, and then to private prayer at all hours. God was close, and the beautiful setting of palm trees, quadrangles, fish ponds, brilliant flowers, arched cloisters, and extensive farm land awakened my heart to the presence of the divine. I began to think about the possibility of a vocation. My parents made it clear that this was *not* an option, and I soon found myself unable to pray or to "be" at home; it was only at school that I felt truly alive....

As I developed a clearer sense of my gifts and of my dreams, I began to experience incredible darkness, especially when it was time to go home for the long summer vacation. With most of my friends having returned to their homes in Libya, Saudi Arabia and England for the summer break, I felt very much alone. From early June until late September, I basically slept away the stifling days, made it to the beach when possible, read extensively and ate all my favorite foods in great quantities. I felt more dead than alive.

Late teens and early adulthood provided some surprises—falling in love for the first time and finding the world temporarily transformed into a garden of delight; having my heart broken so effectively that for two years I refused to believe I would ever recover; falling in love with my husband, Jim, and marrying against my parents' "better judgment"; emigrating to the United States and experiencing major culture shock upon finding myself living in the Back of the Yards, former home of Chicago's stockyards.... I brought my conviction of "deadendedness" with me to the States, as well as my capacity for depression. I brought homesickness and feelings of guilt and confusion; my prayer life was reduced to attending Sunday liturgy and strumming my guitar. God seemed distant; as I moved into married life, I had forgotten the self I used to be....

When I look at the self I have become, when I realize how effectively God has worked with the raw material of my life, when I examine the different areas of ministry with which I am involved, then I have to marvel at God's sense of humor. Here I am—from the tiniest of islands, from a place in which women, until recently, have counted for nothing, from a cultural back-ground rooted in status and materialism—doing "God's work".... Here I am, coming from a history of depression and hopelessness, from the conviction that I was basically "useless," and from a tendency toward dependent relationships and emotional self-absorption, now inspiring others and leading them toward fuller living.... Here I am, with an academic background in "mostly English," teaching theology at all levels, preaching in parishes, preparing clergy for ordination, training laity in spiritual direction.... Here I am, with all my foibles and imperfections, with all the scars and scabs acquired along the way, ready to help others discover their own deepest truth.... Sometimes, when I stop to think of the events which have brought me to the present, I have to laugh heartily; in quieter moments, all I can say is, *"Deo gratias."*

# Private Experience Made Public

Long before I ever conceived of the idea of writing a series of reflections drawn from my own spiritual journey, I was intrigued by the genre of spiritual autobiography. In fact, I had designed and taught an undergraduate class built around Catholic biographies and autobiographies at DePaul University, and had used principles of autobiographical writing in creative writing classes, journal workshops and retreat experiences. Not surprisingly, then, when I saw a seminar listed in the *1993 Parliament of the World Religions'* program on "Spirituality by Means of Autobiography," I enthusiastically penned it into my schedule. The presenter, Reverend Louis Cameli, was a noted spiritual director, author and professor of spirituality at the University of St. Mary of the Lake. His topic, as stated in the program, was to demonstrate how spiritual autobiography is 1) a teaching method of saints and spiritual masters, and 2) a learning tool for anyone on the spiritual path.

Rev. Cameli's starting point was to explore the function of autobiography in the spiritual life. For him, "spiritual experience is personal but not private and, when shared, can be a source of blessing for others." Though such experiences are always unique, "they have a commonality which transcends the particular details —the commonality of divine mystery." Those who record their spiritual journeys reveal the "plot of divine mystery," the fact that our lives "are more than they seem." Spiritual autobiographies, then, reflect the varied ways in which God has taken the initiative in the lives of countless women and men; for Christians, they provide paradigms for our own wrestling with gospel values and our attempt to integrate them into the pattern of daily living.

Cameli's conclusions about the purpose of spiritual autobiography are echoed in a variety of sources. In his basic guide for using the Intensive Journal Process, *At a Journal Workshop*, Ira Progoff comments on the important role the keeping of private journals has played in the history of religion:

> From St. Augustine to Pascal to the Society of Friends, some form of personal journal has been called upon. Sometimes these journals deal with the full range of personal experience including all the intimacies of life from marital quarrels and sexuality to the visionary moments when a person feels himself (sic) to be hovering precariously between prophecy and insanity. Those, of course, are the dramatic journals. But more often the journals deal with an area of religious behavior that is specifically defined by the particular religious group to which the individual belongs. In those cases, the goals set by the sect's beliefs are the basis of keeping the journals. The individual uses the journal as a means of measuring his (sic) progress along the particular religious path he (sic) has chosen. (23-24)

The spiritual autobiography, then, reflects the religious experience of an individual who belongs to a particular group; it provides data about both the individual and the group, while allowing the autobiographer to explore the spiritual dimensions of life more fully. For William James, this personal element in religion is even more significant than ecclesiastical organization or systematic theology: the personal accounts he uses as his data base in *The Varieties of Religious Experience* are the "primordial thing," connecting the reader with voices which reflect a direct encounter with the divine. He writes:

Worship and sacrifice, procedures for working on the dispositions of the deity, theology and ceremony and ecclesiastical organization, are the essentials of religion in the institutional branch. Were we to limit our view to it, we should have to define religion as an external art, the art of winning the favor of the gods. In the more personal branch of religion, it is on the contrary the inner dispositions of man himself (sic) which form the centre of interest, his conscience, his deserts, his helplessness, his incompleteness...the individual transacts the business by himself alone, and the ecclesiastical organization, with its priests and sacraments and other go-betweens, sinks to an altogether secondary place. The relation goes direct from heart to heart, from soul to soul, between man (sic) and his maker. (29)

By examining personal accounts of the human-divine relationship, James is able to offer reflections on the "religion of healthy mindedness" and the "sick soul." His study of the psychology of religion helps the reader to understand such topics as conversion, saintliness, and the mystical journey. The auto-biographical fragments he presents tend to speak for themselves, with little necessity for explication.

Aware of this "usefulness" of spiritual autobiographies in the teaching of world religions to undergraduate college students, Gary L. Comstock describes how he literally "threw away" all his lecture notes on methodology and great religious figures and instead allowed his students to study religious people through the texts they had generated. For students with little prior exposure to religious traditions, spiritual autobiographies helped open them to the experiences of others. Wanting to present a range of powerful and diverse voices and not finding a text to satisfy his criteria, Comstock began assembling his own readings:

....there is no better way to help initiate such understanding than by presenting students with the hopes, fears, memories, and aspirations of others. When students hear the voices of contemporary wayfarers they identify with their struggles and ideals...Something in the narrative unfolding of character makes readers receptive to foreign religious experiences; something about the personal mood of auto-biography makes them want to join the give and take of discussing the stories' meaning and significance. (X)

His textbook, *Religious Autobiographies*, enables the student to "attempt to understand the author's experience as the author understands it," and to raise questions about the narrative (33). This attempt to "cross over" into another's experience heightens the capacity for empathy and provides the occasion for exploring one's own journey, especially in light of the features it shares with other journeys. His selections include paired male and female voices from the worlds of Hinduism, the Lakota Sioux, Zen Buddhism, Judaism, Honduran Catholicism, African-American Protestantism and Islam. The paired stories enable students to identify common themes, but also to note significant differences in the perspectives offered. In this way, they are discouraged from assuming that any single voice can speak for the whole tradition; on the contrary, "Having two stories helps them defeat the natural inclination to take any one story as The Master Story" (XI).

Those who have completed the arduous task of taking pen to paper to record the workings of their inner lives are usually clear about their purpose in writing. St. Augustine's *Confessions*, for example, follows two strategies: the first is to name specifics about Augustine's sinful past; the second is to stress God's goodness and mercy in leading the saint away from error. Beginning with infancy, he points out his greed at his mother's breast, a "sin" that modern Christians may have difficulty accepting unless we are prepared to see this as a sign of "disordered will" common to fallen humanity. He also dwells on sins of childhood, such as his preference for play over studies and for mythology over religion. His robbing of a pear orchard is, for him, another sign of his "perdition" for of what he stole, he already had plenty, "and I had no wish to enjoy the things I coveted by stealing, but only to enjoy the theft itself and the sin" (47). In adolescence and young adulthood, it is his following of the doctrines of the Manichees which leads him astray, as well as his lust and intellectual ambitions. Looking back on his life, then, some ten years after his conversion, he recognizes that he lived a life of sin until he was thirty-two; in fact, it is his understanding that divine grace alone saved him from his own concupiscence. In Book II, he writes:

> I will love you, Lord, and thank you, and praise your name, because you have forgiven me such great sins and such wicked deeds. I acknowledge that it was by your grace I was preserved from whatever sins I did not commit, for there was no knowing what I might have done, since I loved evil even if it served no purpose. (51)

For all her seeming preoccupation with her own status and needs, Margery Kempe (c. 1373-1440 C.E.), author of the earliest known spiritual autobiography in English, offers a similar rationale for recording her experiences. It is difficult to see her book as altruistic in intent, since her main focus seems to be to prove that in spite of having given birth to fourteen children, she is still virginal in the eyes of Christ and that she should therefore wear white garments as a sign of this "virginity." It is this obsession with virginity that leads her to pray for the "slaying" of her husband's sexual desire (56) and which leads her to record the words she claims Christ has revealed to her:

> And because you are a maiden in your soul, I shall take you by the one hand in heaven, and my mother by the other, and so you shall dance in heaven with other holy maidens and virgins, for I may call you dearly bought and my own beloved darling. (88)

Nevertheless, in spite of this "fixed" agenda and her strikingly inflated notions of her own rank, her Proem begins with an explicit statement of purpose:

> Here begins a short treatise and a comforting one for sinful wretches, in which they may have great solace and comfort for themselves, and understand the high and unspeakable mercy of our sovereign Jesus Christ... And therefore, by the leave of our merciful Lord Jesus Christ, to the magnifying of his holy name, Jesus, this little treatise shall treat in part of his wonderful works, how mercifully, how benignly, and how charitably he moved and stirred a sinful wretch to his love.... (33)

In theory, then, if not in fact, the dictated recollections of Margery Kempe were intended to reveal God's wonderful involvement in her life, for God's glory and for the comfort of other Christians.

Julian of Norwich also writes because she feels compelled to do so. Having received a series of sixteen "showings" or visions while she lay dying on May 8th, 1373, she reflects on them for the next twenty years before committing them to writing. In Chapter 8 of *Revelations of Divine Love*, she stresses that what has been shown to her in particular is meant for all in general. She urges the reader to look beyond "the poor wretch who was shown these things" and instead to look at God,

> that in his (sic) loving courtesy and eternal goodness he may be willing to show it to all and sundry, to our own great comfort. For it is God's will that you should receive it with great joy and pleasure, as if Jesus himself had showed it to you all. (74)

And in Chapter 86, the final chapter, she gives God the credit for her book: "This book was begun by the gift and grace of God." For Julian, the revelations were meant not for her own aggrandizement, but for the edification of other Christians that they might come to know something of God's love:

> From the time these things were first revealed I had often wanted to know what was our Lord's meaning. It was more than fifteen years after that I was answered in my spirit's understanding. "You would know our Lord's meaning in this thing? Know it well. Love was his meaning. Who showed it you? Love. What did he show you? Love. Why did he show it? For love." (212)

This goal of mirroring God's goodness by reflecting on one's own life experience is shared by a writer close to our own time. In *The Long Loneliness*, Dorothy Day describes the story of her religious conversion which she wrote twelve years before—a story which left out all her sins, but which outlined those things that had brought her to God. This new book, she assures us, is going to be a "confession":

> Going to confession is hard. Writing a book is hard, because you are "giving yourself away." But if you love, you want to give yourself. You write as you are impelled to write, about man (sic) and his problems, his relation to God and his fellows. You write about yourself because in the long run all man's (sic) problems are the same, his human needs of sustenance and love... I can write only of myself, what I know of myself, and I pray with St. Augustine, "Lord, that I may know myself in order to know Thee." (10-11)

In *From Center to Circumference*, I, too, write only of myself. As I state in the appendix, I did not set out to write a spiritual autobiography but as I drew on more and more of my own story to illustrate the points I was trying to communicate, the book took on a life of its own—a life that was grounded in my life. My stated purpose was to explore the theme of making God the "subject" of my prayer. Cast in the first person, the initial reflection on this topic explains how this invitation originally surfaced. In several highly personal and self-revelatory pages, I allude to family crisis, speak about my prayer life and describe the new sense of call that had emerged in relation to making God "subject."

The pattern was set: style, content, personal examples all seemed to be interwoven; the unifying thread was the theme of allowing God to be both the center and the circumference of self. I began to write—pages here, pages there, as my schedule allowed— simply and succinctly, playing with the spiritual truths which I draw on in my teaching, preaching, retreat work and spiritual direction.

Every now and again, I shared passages with friends and colleagues, only to receive mixed reactions. Some wondered whether it was wise to make so much of my inner life public; others thought it presumptuous for me to write a "spiritual autobiography" because "who on earth would want to read it?" But others were excited by this spiritual "coming out" because they saw it as a source of growth for readers. This positive response was affirmed for me by an elderly woman who wrote to tell me what my writing has meant for her. "For the last five years since I've been a shut in," she said, "I have prayed the rosary daily, listened to tapes and said my other prayers. Now that I've read *Pilgrims at Heart* (Creative Communications, 1993), I realize I don't know what it is to love God...." What had struck her, apparently, was precisely my vulnerability in print.

And so, my intention is more to let the reader reflect on his or her own spiritual journey than to dwell on the events of my life. There is no denying that the book is autobiographical in style, but each event presented points to a universal spiritual truth; it is by no means an end in itself. In the appendix, I go on to explain that one of the guidelines adhered to in spiritual direction is that one should only share one's own experience if it might be "useful" for the directee:

It is my hope that the pieces of myself that have made their way into this book are here because *they* need to be and not because I need them to be. My prayer is that these pieces are "useful."

While my purpose may have been to share with others some of the wisdom I have received along the way, one result for me, personally, is the transformation that comes about in writing about one's own inner life. Writing brings clarity, helps me to make connections, and assists me in being more precise in trying to define and explain that which is beyond words. I found myself stretched and challenged as I looked for appropriate anecdotes to illustrate different topics. Ira Progoff explains the value of perceiving our individual existence and of recognizing "the cycles of change, of development and diminution that comprise our life history": by entering the inner movement of this life history we move beyond a merely intellectual perspective; instead, we actively connect the experiences of our past with the possibilities of the future:

We are dancers joining the dance of our life as it is going on, and continuing it toward its fulfillment. We experience an inner perspective of our life. (13)

# Appendix

Now that this book is ready to make its way into the world, I feel the need to make a disclaimer. There will be those who regard it as autobiography in episode form, but while I cannot deny the fact that *From Center to Circumference: God's Place in the Circle of Self* is autobiographical in style, and is, in fact, very self-revealing, I never intended it to be shelved in the biography section of libraries and book stores. On the contrary, though I draw on my own life experiences, my purpose is not to dwell on the "events of my life," but rather on the spiritual wisdom they illustrate. Moreover, while *my* narrative is a starting point, my hope is that the reader will be drawn to reflect on his or her own spiritual journey.

One of the basic guidelines brought up for spiritual directors in formation programs, seminars and support groups is that one should only share one's own experience if it might be "useful" for the directee. Before embarking on a personal story, those of us who minister as spiritual companions need to check our motives for talking about ourselves: Have we had a similar experience to that of the directee which might shed some light on a particular issue? Will the sharing of our story help the directee to reflect more deeply on this experience and to understand new layers of meaning? Is the sharing of our story simply an exercise in self-indulgence—a filler in of time, an excuse for not listening, an opportunity to process some aspect of our life that still needs healing? Is our personal storytelling intended to enhance our own egos or to bring clarity to the discussion? It is my hope that the pieces of myself that have made their way into this book are here because *they* need to be and not because *I* need them to be. My prayer is that these pieces are "useful."

There are several themes which seem to appear throughout the various chapters. I did not have a "grand scheme" in mind as I wrote, but wrote what came, in the order that it came, drawing on events past and events present. These themes are basic to the spiritual journey in general; some are basic to the Christian journey in particular. They include: allowing God the central place in one's life; surrendering to God; letting go of unhealthy attachments; finding the real self in the Christ-center; and experiencing the traditional stages of the mystical journey— purgation, illumination and union. They are themes which I draw upon in **Fanning the Flame of Faith**, the formation program for lay spiritual companions which I direct for the Archdiocese of Chicago, and in my own ministry of spiritual direction; they are themes I have encountered in my own life, as well as in sacred texts of religions from around the world. They are themes which are "tried and true"; my reflections simply provide them with form.

When I speak of allowing God to be the center and circum- ference of my life, I am not saying anything different than St. Augustine or St. Francis of Assisi or Julian of Norwich or Hadewijch, or, closer to our own time, Etty Hillesum, Dorothy Day, Thomas Merton.... When I write about "surrender," I am in the good company of Muslim saints whose whole way of life is based on submission to Allah, as well as Christians, Jews, Hindus, the followers of Twelve Step programs.... "Letting Go" and "Detachment" bring me to the way of purgation—the Buddhist way, the mystical way, the way of John of the Cross and of all who, like St. Paul, recognize that the false self squeezes out the Real Self, however we define it. My "literary" guides have been as disparate as T.S. Eliot, Aeschylus, Euripides, John

Donne, Evelyn Underhill, Richard Rolle, Walter Hilton, Hildegard of Bingen, Farid Ud-Din Attar, Ewert Cousins, Carol Pearson, Dante, Helen Luke, Abraham Heschel, Alice Walker, Riane Eisler, Mircea Eliade, Joseph Campbell, Carl Jung, Carroll Stuhlmueller C.P.—and I will **not** attempt to link them chronologically, or geographically, or thematically, or even alphabetically, because to do so would be to violate the "wholeness" of their legacy....

And then there are those cherished "unpublished" companions—my personal guides, my friends, my colleagues, those I teach and who, in turn, teach me, those I "direct" who, in turn, "direct me." And then there have been the vicissitudes of life—particularly in family and career—its moments of joy and pain, disappointment and delight, frustration and success....

My intention, then, has not been to provide novelty but to offer the wisdom I have received through my own unique circumstances. That I was born in England and grew up on the island of Malta is irrelevant; that my extended family is spread throughout Europe and also in South Africa is of no consequence; that some of my struggles may have different outcomes than those I believed they would have when writing this book is also beside the point. *From Center to Circumference: God's Place in the Circle of Self* offers a glimpse of the spiritual life; its writer could be Anyone or Nobody, you or me, Everyman or Everywoman—what is important is that God's "authorship" is reflected in its pages....